Pray Like A *Girl*

"Pray P.I.N.K."

*P*ray your way through and praise your way to

*I*ncline your ear to hear and your heart to receive

*N*ever stop believing and trusting in Him

*K*now He will never leave you nor forsake you

PRAYERS FOR "VICTORY" OVER BREAST CANCER

Karen Tate Washington

Pray Like A *Girl*

Cover designed by Karen Tate Washington

ISBN – 978-0-9885664-0-8

Contact:
In His Glory Ministries
Karen Tate Washington
inhisglory2013@yahoo.com

Dedications

This book is dedicated in loving memory of my cousin
Bernadine Tezino
who sings daily her victory song over breast cancer
on the golden streets of heaven.
I can hear her singing
"Victory Is Mine"

Also a special thank you and endless appreciation
to the greatest influence in my life, my Mom,
Elizabeth Sjozet Tizeno, who has taught me courage,
love, compassion, honor and integrity through the
life she lives. Thanks Mom for the sacrifices you made
to protect me, the correction you gave to grow me
and the love you pour out that secures me.
I praise God for the awesome blessing
He has given us in you!
I rise up and call you blessed. (Proverbs 31:28)

Thanks to my husband, Ronald and my daughter,
Maegan for praying for me and supporting me as
God poured Himself out through these pages.
Ronald, thank you for being my Man of Valor and thanks
Maegan my sweetie for your unconditional love, support
and rising up and calling me blessed. (Proverbs 31:28)

Love You Daddy
The Late - David P. Tate Sr.
(*Promise Kept*)

Our Lord God is known as the "Breasted One," because upon His breast we find comfort, nurturing and rest. Satan's attack against women through breast cancer is an attempt to rob us of who God created us to be, nurturers, developers of others, supporters who stand side by side in times of weakness, and comforters who bring soothing ease and rest to a troubled heart. We were created in our Heavenly Father's image and empowered to stand against the wiles, attacks and offenses of the enemy. Remember in the Word of God, the Lord God placed enmity between the woman and her seed and satan and his seed. Enmity is holy indignation, an active hatred, against the author of deception, destruction and disease – the enemy. So let's "Pray Like A Girl", with power, authority, dominion, passion and enmity against satan.

In doing so we must remember that our "Victory" is in knowing who we are in Christ and recognizing the power and authority He has placed in us as overcomers. Then shall we be able to receive the healing He has already paid the ultimate price so that we may walk in it uncompromisingly!

When I was asked to be a team leader for the Breast Cancer Walk, I asked God? What can I do? What can I give to encourage those battling with breast cancer? How can I help them to come to know You in a deeper level as their Healer. And I heard in my heart, His small, still voice saying, "I've already given it to you for a time such as this, now pour it out." As I wrote each prayer, I prayed that you not only experience the healing our Father so desperately longs to bless you with, but also that you and your family walk in a new level of intimacy with Christ that will literally change every aspect of your life. You will come out of this better than you came in – your latter shall be greater than your former.

It is my personal, effectual prayer, that every person that reads this book will be filled with the world changing revelation of who they are in Christ Jesus. I pray that salvation flow through your heart and healing through your body. I declare that what satan meant to use to destroy you, will work to strengthen, establish, perfect and settle you (1 Peter 5:10). I bind and renounce every work of darkness that would come to compete with or challenge the healing power of the Word of God.

The Lord God of Heaven and Earth is your GREAT PHYSICIAN. Receive your healing and tell the world about it!

Karen Tate Washington
Pray Like A Girl and Live Your Life Out Loud

Isaiah 50:4 – The Lord GOD hath given me the tongue of the learned, that I should know how to speak a word in season to him that is weary.

"Pray P.I.N.K."

Table of Contents

A<i>ppendix</i>

Foreword

It was my sincere privilege to write this foreword for "Pray Like A Girl" by Karen Tate Washington. Karen gives a unique perspective on strategic prayer that is both thorough and precise in its approach. Her attention to detail in tackling one of the most urgent challenges of our generation gives women and those who pray for them invaluable spiritual ammunition. This phenomenal compilation of biblical scripture is accompanied with specific measures for total healing of the body, restoration of the mind, and revival of the spirit. This prescription of prayer will empower its beneficiaries with all the necessities for victory and gives even the most casual participant a dynamic repertoire of weapons in the battle against breast cancer. This riveting masterpiece will be a welcome addition to my literary collection and I highly recommend it for you as well!

Ronald L. Mayo, Senior Pastor
United Christian Fellowship Ministries

Prayer for Salvation

Exodus 14:13 – …Fear not, stand still, (firm, confident, undismayed) and see the salvation of the Lord which He will work for you today.

Exodus 15:2 – The Lord is my Strength and my Song, and He has become my Salvation; this is my God, and I will praise Him, my father's God, and I will exalt Him.

2 Samuel 22:3 – My God, My Rock, in Him will I take refuge; my Shield and the Horn of my salvation; my Stronghold and my Refuge, my Savior – You save me…

Psalm 3:8 – Salvation belongs to the Lord; May Your blessing be upon your people.

Psalm 80:3 – Restore us again, O God, and cause Your face to shine (in pleasure and approval on us) and we shall be saved!

Isaiah 38:20 – The Lord is ready to save (deliver) me…

Salvation is accepting God's ultimate act of love, the sacrifice of His Son Jesus Christ on the cross, as the finished work that cleanse you from all sins. Salvation is the surrendering of "self" to Him, allowing Him to fulfill His promises of healing, wholeness and eternal life, in your life. It's receiving His forgiveness so you may live a life that tells the story of His love for you and the world.

The meaning of *salvation* is safety, deliverance, health, aid, prosperity, help and welfare. Allow the Lord God to be all of these to you by giving your life to Him, becoming His child and living His way.

I would like to invite you, if you do not know the Lord Jesus Christ as your personal Lord and Savior, or have turned from Him and are ready to return back to the Arms of the Father, our Healer, to open your heart and receive His Salvation through this prayer. Make Him Lord GOD over your life. His word simply says if you acknowledge and confess with your lips that Jesus is Lord and in your heart believe (adhere to, trust in, and rely on the truth) that God raised Him (Jesus Christ) from the dead; you will be saved (Romans 10:9).

Prayer for Salvation

Heavenly Father I come to You now, knowing that I have sinned and I am a sinner. I accept Your word that promises if I confess my sins that You are faithful and just to forgive me of sin and cleanse me from all unrighteousness. I believe in my heart that You sent Your Son to die for me and He rose from the grave so that I may have eternal life. I ask and receive Your forgiveness and choose today to turn away from sin. I accept You as Lord and Savior of my life. Fill me with Your Holy Spirit and teach me to love Your Word which guides and directs my steps. Help me Lord to work out my salvation daily and to walk in the fullness of Your gift. I am a born again child of God and I thank You Lord. In Jesus name I pray.

If you have invited Jesus into your heart and received Him as your Lord and Savior then you are now a forgiven child of the Most High God and all His promises, including healing and divine health, are now available to you. You must walk out this salvation daily through His word and by joining a bible teaching church who believes in the life changing power of the blood of Jesus. It is vital that you place the word of God into your spirit daily by reading, studying, confessing and living it out in your life day by day. Begin meditating on the scriptures provided with each prayer in this book (see appendix) and watch God move like you never thought imaginable. With God all things are possible.

The Power of God's Word

John 1:1 – In the beginning (before all time) was the Word (Christ) and the Word was with God, and the Word was God, Himself.

Hebrews 4:12 – For the Word that God speaks is alive and full of power (making it active, operative, energizing and effective); it is sharper than any two-edged sword, penetrating to the dividing line of the breath of life (soul) and (the immortal) spirit and of joints and marrow (of the deepest parts of our nature) exposing and sifting and analyzing and judging the very thoughts and purpose of the heart.

James 4:7-8 – Submit yourselves therefore to God. Resist the devil and he will flee from you. Draw nigh (close) to God and He will draw nigh (close) to you.

Ezekiel 11:19 – And I will give them one heart (a new heart) and I will put a new spirit within them and I will take the stony (unnaturally hardened) heart out of their flesh and will give them a heart of flesh sensitive and responsive to the touch of their God.

Psalm 16:11 – You will show me the path of life; in Your presence is fullness of joy, at Your right hand there are pleasures forevermore.

3

Colossians 3:16 – Let the word (spoken by) Christ (the Messiah) have its home (in your hearts and minds) and dwell in you in (all its) richness, as you teach and admonish and train one another on all insight and intelligence and wisdom (in spiritual things and as you sing) psalms and hymns and spiritual songs, making melody to God with (His) grace in your hearts.

The word of God has the supernatural power to renew the mind, comfort the soul, heal the body and change the heart. However, simply reciting the word without building a relationship with God is like trying to build a friendship without the other person. God is His word and it is through His word that you will grow to know Him, love Him, trust Him and believe in Him. As you read, study, speak, think on and pray His word, your heart will become interlocked with His, made tender to His touch, yet strengthened in His love. You will find your heart beating to the same rhythm as His. He takes away our stony heart and gives us His heart (Ezekiel 11:19). As you grow in your relationship with God, and with His word, it will draw you near to Him, to His presence. And in His presence is fullness of joy, healing, peace, rest, comfort, strength, safety and love.

God's word is able to cut through the fears, wounds, hurts, bitterness, shame, guilt, brokenness and the harden places of our hearts. This brings healing to our souls as well as our bodies. Father, create in us a heart that chases after You. A heart that loves Your word and longs to read it, study it, meditate on it, understand it, pray it and live it.

*P*ray Your Way Through
and Praise Your Way To

James 5:13-15 – Is anyone among you afflicted? He should pray. Is anyone glad at heart? He should sing praise (to God). Is anyone among you sick? He should call the church elders (the spiritual guides). And they should pray over him, anointing him with oil in the Lord's name. And the prayer of faith will save him, who is sick, and the Lord will restore him; and if he has committed sins, he will be forgiven.

James 5:16 – Confess to one another therefore your faults (your slips, your false steps, your offenses, your sins) and pray for one another, that you may be healed and restored (to the spiritual tone of mind and heart). The earnest (heartfelt, continued) prayer of a righteous (one in right standing with God) man (availeth) makes tremendous power available (dynamic in its working).

Jeremiah 17:14 – Heal me, O Lord, and I shall be healed; save me and I shall be saved, for You are my praise!

Romans 4:20 – No unbelief or distrust made him waver (doubtingly question) concerning the promise of God, but he "grew" strong and was empowered by faith as he gave praise and glory to God…

Isaiah 12:5 – Sing praises to the Lord, for He has done excellent things (gloriously); let this be made known to all the earth.

Psalm 96:4 – For great is the Lord and greatly to be praised; He is to be reverently feared and worshiped above all …

Prayer and praise are our spiritual weapons against every attack that the enemy makes against us. Prayer is how we communicate with the Lord. We speak to Him and He speaks to us. It's a time of communion, supplication, confession, petitioning, hearing, and building our relationship with God. The more you pray the closer you become to the Lord who is your Healer. Prayer changes things and equips you for the battles you will face.

Praise and worship always finds place in the heart of the Father. We were created to praise Him. Our hearts are turned to Him as we praise and we draw near to the True and Living God. Praise supernaturally destroys the enemy's (satan's) strongholds in our mind, body and soul leaving him ineffective in our lives.

Prayer and Praise Confession
Thank You Lord, for depositing in me the ability to pray prayers that availeth much and praises that destroys strongholds. I will praise You in the good times and praise You in my time of trouble because You are the Lord God that healeth me. Father I expect to hear Your small, still voice in my prayers and remain alert and attentive to Your direction as You whisper to me. I am growing daily in my prayer power through Your word and Your Presence. Your word promises that if I ask, with believing, then I will have what I ask. I ask You to fill me with Your Holy Spirit and empower me with a passion for prayer and a heart of praise. Teach me Lord, how to effectually pray and lead me Father into a new dimension of praise that I may show forth Your marvelous works. I praise You, I lift up Your Holy Name, I exalt, reverence and worship You, for You are truly worthy of all my praise! In Jesus name I pray. Amen.

Prayer for Healing

Ephesians 4:23 – And be constantly renewed in the spirit of your mind (having a fresh mental and spiritual attitude).

Isaiah 53:5 – He was wounded for our transgressions, He was bruised for our iniquities; the chastisement of our peace was upon Him, and with His stripes we are healed.

Romans 8:10 – But if Christ is in me, the body is dead because of sin, but the Spirit is alive because of righteousness. And if the Spirit of Him who raised Jesus from the dead dwells in me, He who raised Christ from the dead will also give life to my mortal body through the Spirit who dwells in me!

Exodus 23:25-26 – You shall serve the Lord your God, He shall bless your bread and water, and I will take sickness away from the midst of thee…the number of thy days I will fulfill.

Psalm 103:2-3 – Bless the Lord oh my soul and forget not all His benefits; Who forgive all thy iniquities, Who healeth all my diseases.

Jeremiah 30:17 – For I will restore health unto thee, and I will heal thee of thy wounds, saith the Lord.

Psalm 107:20 – He sends forth His word and heals them and rescues them from the pit and destruction.

Psalm 30:2 – O Lord my God, I cried to You and You have healed me.

Mark 10:52 – And Jesus said to him, Go your way; your faith has healed you.

1 Peter 2:24 – He personally bore our sins in His (own) body on the tree (as on an altar and offered Himself on it) that we might die (cease to exist) to sin and live to righteousness. By His wounds you have been HEALED.

Ephesians 3:20 – Now to Him, Who by (in consequence of) the [action of His] power that is at work within us, is able to [carry out His purpose and] do superabundantly, far over and above all that we [dare] ask or think [infinitely beyond our highest prayers, desires, thoughts, hopes or dreams.]

3 John 1:2 – Beloved, I pray that you may prosper in every way and (that your body) may keep well, even as (I know) your soul (your mind, will and emotions) keeps well and prospers.

The thoughts you think produce the words you speak. The words you speak feed into the thoughts you think resulting in the actions you take. This process can become either a vicious cycle of defeat or a victorious cycle of victory. God's word tells us that as a man thinketh so is he (Proverbs 23:7) and that the power of life and death is in the tongue (Proverbs 18:21). Therefore, our healing is connected to the thoughts we think, the words we speak and the actions that result. The word of God has the supernatural power to renew your thinking and build your faith. Faith comes by hearing, and hearing by the word of God (Romans 10:17).

Jesus is known as the "Balm of Gilead". In biblical times, balm was used to bring healing, soothing and preservation. The city of Gilead had a plentiful supply of the tree in which the balm was extracted from and exported it to the world. Jesus Christ is the Balm - The Healer – that has an endless supply of healing for the world and for you.

Healing is part of the wonderful gift of salvation. It is a completed work, the finished fruit of Jesus' sacrifice on the cross. You are not trying to be healed –you are healed. To receive salvation you must confess with your mouth and believe in your heart (Romans 10:9) …if you acknowledge and confess with your lips that Jesus is Lord and in your heart believe (adhere to, trust in, and rely on the truth) that God raised Him from the dead, you will be saved. You receive healing in the same manner. You must confess with your mouth "I am healed" and believe in your heart, "I am healed". Again you are not trying to be healed or trying to get healing, you "are" (present tense) already healed. You must believe this in your heart, think it in your thoughts, speak it out of your mouth and trust God to manifest it through your body. Your life mirrors your words.

Prayer
Heavenly Father, I thank You for my healing and wholeness. I am the healed protecting my health from sickness and disease. Cancer you cannot lord over my body or my mind. I am filled with the knowledge of the Lord's will and His will is for me to prosper and be in "good health" as my soul (mind, will, and emotions) prospers. The blood of Jesus has healed my body and has delivered me from the darkness of sin. My Lord and Savior, Jesus Christ took thirty-nine stripes on His back so that I could walk in divine health and healing and I receive His gift of healing now by faith.

I declare Your word, that is alive and powerful, over my body, and accept it as true, that by the stripes of Jesus who God raised from the dead, I AM HEALED. From the very crown of my head to the soul of my feet I am whole, complete, healthy, nothing missing, nothing broken, healed and set free from cancer and every disease, infection, germ, or virus.

I refuse to accept anything less. For my God is more than able to do exceedingly, abundantly above and beyond all that I can ask or think according to the power (His word, the Holy Spirit, His love) that works in me. (Eph. 3:20). I praise You Lord, I praise You and trust You. I confidently pray in Jesus name.

❧ ✳✳✳✳✳✳✳✳✳✳✳✳✳✳✳✳✳✳✳✳✳✳✳✳✳✳✳✳✳✳✳✳✳✳✳✳✳✳✳ ☙

Healing Communion

Mark 14:22-24 – And while they were eating, He took a loaf (bread), praised God and gave thanks and asked Him to bless it to their use. Then He broke it and gave to them and said, Take. Eat. This is My body. He also took a cup (of juice of grapes) and when He had given thanks, He gave it to them and they all drank of it. And He said to them, This is My blood (which ratifies) the new covenant, (the blood) which is being poured out for many for forgiveness of sins.

1 Corinthians 10:16-17 – The cup of blessing (of wine at the Lord's Supper) upon which we ask (God's) blessing, does it not mean (that in drinking it) we participate in and share a fellowship (a communion) in the blood of Christ (the Messiah)? The bread which we break, does it not mean (that in eating it) we participate in and share a fellowship (a communion) in the body of Christ? For we (no matter how) numerous we are, are one body, because we all partake of the one Bread (the One Whom the communion bread represents).

1 Corinthians 11:23-26 – For I received from the Lord Himself that which I passed on to you, that the Lord Jesus on the night when He was treacherously delivered up and

while His betrayal was in progress took bread, and when He had given thanks, He broke it and said, Take, Eat. This is My body, which is broken for you. Do this to call Me (affectionately) to remembrance. For every time you eat this bread and drink this cup, you are representing and signifying and proclaiming the fact of the Lord's death until He comes (again).

1 Corinthians 11:28 – Let a man (thoroughly) examine himself, and (only when he has done) so should he eat of the bread and drink of the cup.

1 Peter 2:24 – He personally bore our sins in His (own) body on the tree (the cross – as on an altar and offered Himself on it) that we might die (cease to exist) to sin and live to righteousness (in right standing, communion with God). By His wounds you have been healed.

1 John 1:9 – If we (freely) admit that we have sinned and confess our sins, He is faithful and just (true to His own nature and promises) and will forgive our sins (dismiss our lawlessness) and (continuously) cleanse us from all unrighteousness (everything not in conformity to His will in purpose, thought, and action).

Taking communion acknowledges and brings to our remembrance that awesome act of love our Lord gave us by giving His life so that we could live. Taking on our sins, our sickness, our iniquities and becoming the Divine Ultimate Sacrifice that paid the cost (IN FULL) for every sin we have or could ever commit. He paid our debt that we may be forgiven, redeemed, healed and have eternal life with our Father in Heaven. Daily communion with God cleanses your mind, body and soul. Communion represents the union between us and the Lord GOD we serve. It is the intimate fellowship with our Father, the Great Physician, our Strong Tower and Ever Present Help in times of trouble. It creates a place of oneness with the Almighty where we truly come to recognize, accept and trust that His blood unquestionably washed away all our sins and His body which was sacrificed for us, has healed us.

When taking communion daily, begin by meditating on the scriptures mentioned; asking the Holy Spirit for understanding, insight and revelation (which He will reveal more and more each day). Follow, with the Holy Spirit as your guide, a search of your heart for anything (sins, un-forgiveness, bitterness, fear…) that is not of God and ask the Lord's forgiveness (1 Corinthians 11:28 – Let a man (thoroughly) examine himself, and (only when he has done) so should he eat of the bread and drink of the cup). He is faithful and just to forgive those sins that you confess and throw them into the sea of forgetfulness. Also ask the Lord for the grace to forgive those that have offended and wounded you that you may also be forgiven. Finally, lift up your hands and praise the Lord GOD with the fruit of your lips for He is truly worthy. Offer Him your sacrifice of praise. Take communion daily (juice of grapes – that represents the blood of Jesus and bread – that represents the body of Christ) as you receive your healing.

Prayer
Father search my heart and if there is anything that is not of You, I pray that You remove it so I may commune with You with all my heart. I humbly ask You to forgive me of _____ or any sins that I have unknowingly committed. Thank You for faithfully forgiving me and I receive Your forgiveness.

I now take this Communion in remembrance of You. Thank You for being my substitutionary sacrifice on the cross and taking on my sins. Thank You for Your Blood that cleanse me and Your body that was broken, so I could walk in Divine Health. Every disease, germ, virus, infection, or cancer that touches my body dies instantly in the name of the Lord Jesus Christ whom I believe in and diligently put my trust. Jesus already paid the price for my body to be healed and I receive right now the victory of His sacrifice. I give praise to You and offer up a sacrifice of thanksgiving. I praise You for who You are. I praise You for being my Healer. I praise You Lord, for the sacrifice You made. I will praise You in the good times and I will praise You in the struggle. For You are my Redeemer. In Jesus mighty name I pray.

Prayer of Intercession for Others

Job 42:10 – And the Lord turned the captivity of Job and restored his fortunes, when he prayed for his friends; also the Lord gave twice as much as he had before.

Romans 8:27 – And He Who searches the hearts of men knows what is in the mind of the (Holy) Spirit, because the Spirit intercedes and pleads (before God) in behalf of the saints …

Isaiah 59:16 – And He (the Lord God) saw that there was no man and wondered that there was no intercessor…

Intercession is your prayers on behalf of another; standing in the gap. What you make happen for others, God will make happen for you. Begin to sow in prayer for another and reap the blessings of intercession. In difficult times of

13

trouble, praying for others will bear fruit in your situation. God seeks for one that will stand in the gap on behalf of others and allow Him to pour out His Spirit upon them. Jesus Christ is our Intercessor, praying on our behalf in heaven and we are God's workmanship here on earth to do as Jesus does – intercede for others.

Find someone who is struggling with your same struggle and begin to pray fervently for them from your heart and watch God flood you with His Presence and move on your behalf.

Prayer

Father I come before You to lift up _____ and pray on their behalf. I ask You to bless them with Your peace that surpasses all understanding. I ask You Father to go into the very recesses of their heart and heal all brokenness and bring healing to their body. I pray that Your joy overtake them and Your Presence overshadow any fear or doubt. Send salvation into their home and bless their family. Help them to trust in You with all of their heart and not to waver in their belief. Thank You Lord for meeting their every need and giving them the desires of their heart. Show them Your abundance of love and use me as a source of encouragement to them. Give me kind words to speak and warm hugs to share. Continue to place them on my heart throughout the day and prompt my spirit to intercede on their behalf. I praise You right now for their healing and wholeness! Hallelujah.

Prayer for Your Husband

Ephesians 4:32 – Be kind to one another, tenderhearted, forgiving one another, even as God in Christ forgave you.

Psalm 90:17 – Let the beauty of the Lord our God be upon us; and establish the works of our hands for us; yes, establish the works of our hands.

Philippians 2:1-2 (KJV) – If there is any consolation in Christ, if any comfort of love, if any fellowship of the Spirit, if any affection and mercy. Fulfill my joy by being like-minded, having the same love, being of one accord, of one mind.

Isaiah 41:10 – Fear not, I am with you; be not dismayed, for I am your God. I will strengthen you, yes, I will help you, I will uphold you with My righteous right hand.

God has ordained our husbands as the priest of our home, the provider of our needs and the protector of our families. Their position as priest of the home, regardless if they are in position or not, deposits in them (even unknowingly) an ability to pray prayers that bring change. As providers, they carry the responsibility of assuring that the needs of the family are met and as protectors they want to fix whatever is wrong. Our husbands think differently than us, express themselves differently than us, cope and process differently than us. However, regardless of the differences, they hold the key to our hearts and are a vital part of our healing. Their position of priest, provider and protector can become very burdensome and weighty if they try to carry it without the Lord.

Prayer
Lord help my husband _____ as the priest of our home to lean on You and to go to You in prayer when he feels helpless and loss for words. Help him to speak life and to meditate on Your word for comfort, guidance and direction. Teach my husband Father, how not to bear the

weight of this battle on his shoulders but allow the eyes of his understanding to be enlightened that he may see that You are our Healer and our Protector.

Thank You Jesus for establishing the works of his hands, so that he shall not have to struggle with providing the needs of our family. Give him the heart of a giver and tither that our finances may be blessed.

I pray that he draws closer and closer to You and develops a Father - son relationship that changes his life and empowers him to be the man that You created him to be. Show me how to love him in a way that he can receive, understand and embrace. Strengthen our love walk with each other and You which brings healing and wholeness to my body, our marriage and our family. Grow and unite us into one flesh that is strengthened and fortified in You. Give us patience with one another and compassion for each other as we defeat the enemy together. Open us up to forgive each other of any offenses, hurts or wounds that we may have knowingly or unknowingly inflicted on each other in our marriage so that our love walk cannot be hindered. Take away any fears that may try to take up residency in his thinking and help him to express his emotions and to release them. Send godly men into his life that he can safely share and express his feelings and concerns. I declare that the Spirit of the Lord is upon my husband _____ the spirit of council and might, the spirit of wisdom, and understanding and the fear (reverence and honor) of the Lord. My husband is a mighty man of valor, the priest of our home, the provider of our needs and the protector of my heart. In Jesus matchless name I pray.

Prayer for Your Children

Psalm 34:11 – Come, you children, listen to me: I will teach you to revere and worshipfully fear the Lord.

Proverbs 14:26 – In the reverent and worshipfully fear of the Lord there is strong confidence and His children shall always have a place of refuge.

Proverbs 20:7 – The righteous man walks in his integrity, blessed (happy, fortunate, enviable) are his children after him.
Proverbs 31:28 – Her children rise up and call her blessed (happy, fortunate, and to be envied)…

Philippians 1:6 – Being confident of this very thing, that He which hath begun a good work in you will perform it until the day of Jesus Christ.

John14:13-14 – Whatever you ask in My Name, that I will do, that the Father may be glorified in the Son. If you ask anything in My Name, I will do it.

As a mother struggling in your body, you must learn how to release your children into the capable hands of God and allow them to remain in the safety of His arms. Accept helping hands from friends and family in caring for your children while you are receiving your healing. God will place people into your path to assist you and for you to lean on in times of need.

A mother's value far exceeds what she does. It's the "who" she is, that makes her the nurturing loving presence that her children know, feel, and love, even when she is not able to "do" the things a mother does. Never doubt the power of a praying mother that protects, warns, covers, secures and dispatches angels to watch over her children. Our prayers are birthed in the depths of our hearts and connected to the heart of the Father, which has more protective power than we could ever provide for our children in the natural realm.

I know with confidence that my present, victorious walk with Christ and the anointing on my life was birthed and nurtured through my mother's prayers. When I was a little girl, prayers were prayed over me and my siblings by our Mom as she lay in the bed of affliction defeating cancer twice. She was unable to care for us for months being confined to a hospital, but her prayers crossed over every barrier that separated us from her and covered, protected and secured us for a life time. I thank God for my praying Mom whose prayers from years gone by are still producing fruit that remains. So "Pray Like A Girl" mothers and trust that your Father in heaven hears your prayers and is placing angels on assignment to care for your children. Trust in Him with all your heart.

Prayer
Dear Lord, I thank You that no evil shall befall my child(ren) nor shall any plague come nigh to them. I know and confidently trust that You have placed Your angels to watch over them, to keep them and protect them. Thank You in advance for sending godly people into my life that will stand in the gap and help care for my child(ren) when I need to restore and recover. My child(ren) are my blessing and they rise up and call me blessed. I stand as a "Praying Mother" and declare that no weapon formed against my child(ren) can prosper.

My child(ren), _____ are blessed and highly favored, the head and not the tail, overcomers and trailblazers.

They shall fulfill their spiritual destiny and walk up rightly before You all the days of their life.

I celebrate that my child(ren) are accepted in the Beloved and they know who they are in Christ. They shall not be deceived by the deceptions of these times, but walk in wisdom, understanding, integrity and divine purpose. My child(ren) shall worshipfully fear (reverence and honor) the Lord God and blessed shall be their path. As for me and my house, we will serve the Lord and great shall be our peace. In Jesus name. Amen.

❧ ** ☙

Prayer for Family Unity

Proverbs 24:3-4 – Through wisdom a house is built and by understanding it is established, by knowledge the rooms are filled with all precious and pleasant riches.

Acts 16:31 – …Believe in the Lord Jesus Christ (giving yourself up to Him, take yourself out of your own keeping and entrust yourself into His keeping) and you will be saved (and this applies both to) you and your household as well.

Proverbs 13:22 – A good man leaves an inheritance (of moral stability and goodness) to his children's children…

Matthew 18:20 (KJV) – For where two or more are gathered together in My name, there Am I in the midst of them.

Joshua 24:15 – …as for me and my house, we will serve the Lord.

A family that prays together stays together. The unity of a praying family creates a hedge of protection and a fortified wall around you and yours. Salvation brings wholeness to you individually, as well as wholeness to the family unit. When a household is on one accord, the enemy can't penetrate, divide or hinder the move of God on behalf of that family. You will need the power of unity in this battle and your family can be that place of power through oneness in heart and prayer.

Prayer

I pray Merciful Father that You will bring my family into a place of unity and strength. I thank You in advance, believing and knowing that it is Your will for my household to be saved and united. In Your word, You promised that You would take what satan meant for evil and work it for good. I ask You to take this attack against my body and use it to unite my family in Your word and through Your healing powers. Teach us Lord how to walk in agreement and maintain the unity You are bringing to my household. Lead us and guide us into Your truths so we are able to quickly identify and remove anything or anyone that threatens to bring division into our family. Give us a heart to pray together that we may build a prayer wall that protects the unity of our household and withstands the attacks of the enemy. In Jesus name I pray.

Prayer of Praise

Psalm 22:3 (KJV) – But thou art Holy, O Thou, that inhabits the praises of Israel (His people).

Psalm 18:49 – Therefore will I give thanks and extol You, O Lord, among the nations, and sing praises to Your Name.

2 Samuel 22:4 – I call on the Lord, Who is worthy to be praised, and I am saved from my enemies.

1 Chronicles 16:25 – Great is the Lord and greatly to be praised. He is to be honored, and given glory above all others and above all else.

The word *praise* means to glorify, celebrate, exalt and magnify. God created us to praise Him. He moves supernaturally when He hears the heartfelt praises of His people. Our praises are a sweet aroma in the nostrils of our Almighty God and it brings great pleasure to His ears to hear the sound of our voices as we celebrate Him. Healing takes place in praise. As you abandon yourself in praise, the very windows of heaven are opened and God pours out His blessings and glory upon you. Celebrate your healing in praise and dancing before the Lord and He will come down, inhabit, and take up residence in your praise! Lose yourself in His presence, open your mouth and praise Your Savior who sent His word and healed you.

Prayer
I will bless Your Holy name, My Lord, for You are truly worthy to be praised. I thank You for my healing and praise You in the midst. Inhabit and dwell in my praises Lord as I lift my hands in reverence of Who You are and the miracle working power of Your presence. Help me to praise You in everything I do and every challenge I face. My praise is a weapon of warfare against the enemy that renders him powerless and defeated in my life. I was created to praise You and Your praises will continuously be in my mouth. In the midst of this attack, yet will I glorify You through my praise, leaving the enemy confused, dethrowned and baffled by the power of my praise. Amen and Amen.

*I*ncline Your Ear to Hear and Your Heart to Receive

Proverbs 4:20-22 – My son, attend to my words, incline thine ear unto My saying. Let them not depart from thine eyes; keep them in the midst of thine heart. For they are life unto those that find them, and health to all their flesh.

Psalm 10:17 (KJV) – Lord, thou hast heard the desire of the humble; thou wilt prepare their heart, thou wilt cause thine ear to hear.

Psalm 54:2-4 (KJV) – Hear my prayer, O God; give ear to the words of my mouth…Behold, God is mine helper, the Lord is with them that uphold my soul.

Job 22:22 – Receive, I pray you, the law and instruction from His mouth and lay up His words in your heart.

Psalm 51:10 – Create in me a clean heart, O God and renew a right, persevering, and steadfast spirit within me.

Psalm 139:23-24 – Search me (thoroughly), O God, and know my heart! Try me and know my thoughts! And see if there is any wicked or hurtful way in me, and lead me in the way everlasting.

Proverbs 5:1 – My son be attentive to My Wisdom (godly Wisdom learned by actual and costly experience) and incline your ear to My understanding.

The Lord requires that we have an ear to hear and a heart to receive His instructions, His directions, and His Word, that carries within it the power to heal. If we are not able to receive the gift of healing, then we will only know of it and never possess it. We must ask the Father to create in us clean hands and a pure heart that we may be open and able to receive all the wonderful blessings He has for us. The blessings of healing, wholeness, joy, peace, prosperity, completeness, confidence in Christ and a life filled continuously with victory. We must allow God to look into our hearts and into our thoughts to find those hindrances that may lay dormant in the very recesses of our being. Then allow Him to remove them so that we may hear His voice and have a heart that is able to receive all that He has for us.

Prayer

I come to You Lord with a humble heart and ask for You to create in me a heart that is open and ready to receive Your instructions, Your comfort, Your healing, and Your love. I ask You to search me, know me, try me, and examine my heart and my thoughts. If there be any unrighteous thing in me, remove it and cleanse me of it, that I may be able to receive Your Healing, Your Wholeness, Your Peace and Your Joy. Father go into the hidden places of my heart, that sub-conscious part of me that I am not even aware of and uproot everything that would deafen my ears from hearing Your voice or harden my heart from receiving all that Your salvation affords me – safety, deliverance, health, healing, aid, prosperity, help and welfare. I pray in Jesus name, Amen.

Morning Prayer of Encouragement

Psalm 5:3 – In the morning You hear my voice, O Lord; in the morning I prepare (a prayer, a sacrifice) for You and watch and wait (for You to speak to my heart).

Lamentations 3:22-23 – It is because of the Lord's mercy and loving-kindness that we are not consumed, because His (tender) compassions fail not. They are new every morning; great and abundant is Your stability and faithfulness.

Psalm 27:14 – Wait and hope for and expect the Lord; be brave and of good courage and let your heart be stout (bold) and enduring. Yes, wait for and hope for and expect the Lord.

2 Corinthians 1:3-4 – Blessed be the God and Father of our Lord Jesus Christ, the Father of sympathy (pity and mercy) and the God (Who is the Source) of every comfort (consolation and encouragement), Who comforts (consoles and encourages) us in every trouble (calamity and affliction), so that we may also be able to comfort (console and encourage) those who are in any kind of trouble or distress, with the comfort (consolation and encouragement) with which we ourselves are comforted, encouraged by God.

How you start your morning sets the tone for the rest of your day. Matthews 6:33 says, "Seek ye first the kingdom of God and His righteousness and all these things will be added unto you." The morning is the beginning and the most peaceful time of the day. God loves to meet with us in the morning before the distractions or busyness of life can capture our attention. The morning is a special time in which you can meet quietly with your Heavenly Father, speak to Him face to face as a man does his friend and allow Him to deposit into your heart His overwhelming love for you. Take the mornings as your opportunity to sit with your Healer, your Comforter, your Encourager and watch as His Presence takes you into an indescribable place of security and oneness with the Almighty.

Prayer

O Father, sometimes my days become so challenging and so difficult I don't know where to turn. But You knew I would face what I am facing and You sent Your word to be my personal comforter, encourager and my place of assurance. Thank You for meeting me in the mornings. I will rise up early and speak Your word over my life. Strengthen me Lord that I may come face to face with You as a man does his friend. You call me friend and I long to sit with You and hear Your Voice. I will rise in the morning and declare life over my body, joy in my heart and peace in my mind. Today is the day that You have made and I will rejoice and be glad in it. I am expecting something good to happen to me this day! I pray in Jesus name.

Right Confessions – My Words Shape My Life

Proverbs 18:21 – Death and life are in the power of the tongue, and they who indulge in it shall eat the fruit of it.

Psalm 141:3 – Set a guard, O Lord, before my mouth, keep watch at the door of my lips.

Psalm 30:12 – To the end, my tongue and my heart and everything glorious within me may sing praises to You and not be silent. O Lord, my God I will give thanks to You forever.

Proverbs 12:18 – There are those who speak rashly, like the piercing of a sword, but the tongue of the wise brings healing.

1 Peter 3:10 – For let him who wants to enjoy life and see good days keep his tongue free from evil and his lips from deceit.

Philippians 2:11 – And every tongue confess and acknowledge that Jesus Christ is Lord, to the glory of God the Father.

Proverbs 18:20 – A man's (moral) self shall be filled with the fruit of his mouth; and with the consequences of his words he must be satisfied (whether good or bad).

Romans 10:9-10 – …confess with your lips…and in your heart believe…with the heart a person believes…and with the mouth he confesses.

Psalm 63:3 – O Lord open my lips and my mouth shall show forth Your praise.

The words we speak will shape our lives. Making the right confessions is a vital part to your healing and the maintaining of that healing. The word of God says that the power of death and the power of life are in our tongues (Proverbs 18:21). What are you speaking over your body, your family, your finances, your faith…? What you are expecting must line up with the words you speak. There is a direct connection between what you confess out of your lips and what you believe in your heart. The tongue is untamed and must be bridled.

Begin taking an inventory of the words you speak and examine if they are words that are in line with the word of God and His plans for your life. You must look at your situation and "speak" those things, not as you see them, but as you want, believe and expect to see them through

God's capable hands. Speak LIFE – speak the word of God regardless of what you feel or see. And as you speak forth life, your heart will begin to believe the words that you are depositing there. Don't speak the problem, speak the answer – the word of God is that answer. Our lips were created to worship, to praise His marvelous name, to share the good news of the gospel and to speak life into others and ourselves. When you are in right standing with the Lord, living according to His instructions and rooting His word into your heart, than shall you decree and speak forth a thing and it shall be established for you, and the light of God's favor shall shine upon your ways.

Prayer

Lord, I ask that You set guard over my mouth and keep watch at the door of my lips that I may speak life not death, healing not sickness, and joy not sorrow. I thank You for the help You have sent me through Your word. I will take Your word daily and renew my thinking so the words that proceed from my mouth and deposit into my heart will prove to be worthy and acceptable in Your sight. Let me speak to my mountain without doubting, and see it casted into the sea and speak life to dead situations and see them breathe again.

I believe that the power of both life and death are in the tongue and I choose to speak life. I choose to speak health and divine healing over my body. Lord, set a Holy Ghost siren in my spirit that will sound an alarm every time I speak a word that does not align with Your word and will for my life and my healing. My lips shall continuously speak forth praises of Your miraculous healing power and Your endless love for me. I pray in the matchless name of Jesus.

Prayer for Wisdom and Understanding

Ephesians 1:17 – For I always pray to the God of our Lord Jesus Christ, the Father of glory, that He may grant you a spirit of wisdom and revelation in the knowledge of Him.

Ephesians 1:18 – By having the eyes of your heart flooded with light so that you can know and understand the hope to which He has called you and how rich is His glorious inheritance in the saints (His set apart ones).

James 1:5 – If any of you is deficient in wisdom, let him ask of the giving God (Who gives) to everyone liberally and ungrudging, without reproaching of faultfinding and it will be given him.

Job 12:12-13 – With the aged (you say) is wisdom and with the length of days comes understanding. But only with God are (perfect) wisdom and might; He alone has (true) counsel and understanding.

Our Heavenly Father says that if anyone is in need of wisdom then He will willfully give it to them. Pray for God to give you wisdom, insight and understanding about the things you do not understand. God's wisdom reveals and discerns things that man's wisdom will never comprehend. It has always been hidden in Christ Jesus and revealed only to those that elect to follow Him. This Godly understanding brings assurance and calm even in the midst of a roaring storm. He says, "Wisdom is the principle thing; therefore get wisdom: and with all thy getting get understanding" (Proverbs 4:7 - KJV). You will be faced with many things that you will not understand and be required to make decisions you would prefer not to have to confront. However, the wisdom of God will lead and guide you every step of the way and His understanding will be a comforter on which you can lean.

Prayer

Heavenly Father, I come before You seeking to understand what makes little sense to me in this trying time. I have many unanswered questions, many whys and many how comes. I need your wisdom that gives me peace in unexplainable circumstances, Your revelation that shines light into dark places, so that I may find rest in the most unexpected situations. Your word says that wisdom is a defense (Ecclesiastes 7:12), that shields and preserves the life of him who has it. I ask that You send Your winds of wisdom into my life and shower me with Your understanding that I may stand firm even in this trial. In Jesus name I pray. Amen.

Grace to Endure

2 Corinthians 12:9 – My grace (My favor and loving-kindness and mercy) is enough for you (sufficient against any danger and enables you to bear the trouble) for My Strength and Power are made perfect (fulfilled and completed) and show themselves most effective in (your) weakness and infirmities, that the strength and power of Christ (the Messiah) may rest (yes, pitch a tent over and dwell) upon you.

Hebrews 4:16 – Let us then fearlessly and confidently and boldly draw near to the throne of grace (the throne of God's unmerited favor) that we may receive mercy (for our failures) and find grace to help in good time for every need (appropriate help and well-timed help, coming just when we need it).

Psalm 121:1-2 – I will lift my eyes to the hills from whence shall my help come. My help comes from the Lord, Who made heaven and earth.

2 Timothy 2:3 – Thou therefore endure hardness, as a good solider of Jesus Christ.

James 4:6 – But He gives more and more grace (power of the Holy Spirit, to meet this evil tendency and all other fully)…God gives grace (continually) to the lowly (those who are humble enough to receive it).

Ephesians 1:2 – May grace (God's unmerited favor) and spiritual peace (which means peace with God and harmony, unity, and undisturbness) be yours from God our Father and from the Lord Jesus Christ.

Grace is God's unmerited favor given simply because of Who He is and not what we have earned. It is His favor (aid, assistance) for whatever you are facing, that gives you the ability to stand. It's divine assistance given by the Father to do and endure that which we do not have the power to bear on our own. Lean on God to carry you through, and pull from His endless supply of endurance. He will give you the grace; ability – to endure and withstand. God's grace is sufficient (enough to meet the needs of your situation) if you are humble enough to receive it.

Prayer

Almighty God I ask that You blanket me with Your grace that I may stand against the wiles of the enemy. I receive Your unmerited favor, which brings a peace that surpasses my understanding. I confess that Your grace is sufficient to take me through to my victory. Thank You Father that through Your salvation I have been equipped to endure this battle and overcome by the blood of Jesus. When I am weary, I will look to the hills from which my help comes. My help comes from You and Your grace empowers me to move forward even in difficult times. I pray in the name of Jesus.

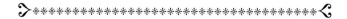

Forgiveness - Healing for the Soul Overcoming Anger, Bitterness and Offense

Psalm 31:2-3 – Bow down Your ear to me, deliver me speedily! Be my Rock of refuge, a strong Fortress to save me! Yes, You are my Rock and my Fortress, therefore for Your name's sake lead me and guide me.

Ephesians 4:31-32 – Let all bitterness and indignation and wrath (passion, rage, bad temper) and resentment (anger, animosity) and quarreling…be banished from you… And become useful and helpful and kind to one another, tenderhearted (compassionate, understanding, loving-hearted), forgiving one another (readily and freely), as God in Christ forgave you.

Proverbs 14:29 – He who is slow to anger has great understanding…

James 1:19 – Understand (this), my beloved brethren. Let every man be quick to hear (a ready listener), slow to speak, slow to take offense and to get angry.

Psalm 147:3 – He heals the brokenhearted and binds up their wounds (curing their pains and their sorrows).

Hebrews 12:15 – Exercise foresight and be on the watch to

look (after one another), to see no one falls back from and fails to secure God's grace (his unmerited favor and spiritual blessing) in order that no root of resentment (rancor, bitterness, or hatred) shoots forth and causes trouble and bitter torment, and the many become contaminated and defiled by it.

1 Timothy 2:8 – I desire therefore that in every place men should pray, without anger or quarreling or resentment or doubt (in their minds) lifting up holy hands.

Matthew 6:14-15 – For if you forgive people their (offenses) trespasses, (their reckless and willful sins, leaving them, letting them go, and giving up resentment), your Father will also forgive you.

Mark 11:26 – But if you do not forgive, neither will your Father in heaven forgive your failings and shortcomings.

Psalm 4:4 –Be angry but sin not; commune with your own heart (do a self-inventory) upon your bed and be silent (sorry for the things you say in your hearts). Selah (pause, and calmly think of that)!

Proverbs 19:11 – Good sense makes a man restrain his anger and it is his glory to overlook a transgression or an offense.

Ephesians 4:26-27 – When you are angry do not sin; do not ever let your wrath (your exasperation, your fury or indignation) last until the sun goes down. Leave no (such) room or foothold for the devil (give no opportunity to him).

Un-forgiveness is the cancer of the soul. It grows and spreads and takes life from everything it touches. It will grow undetected in our hearts and mind as it creates a path of destruction. Un-forgiveness produces stress each time you think (replay) the offense which compromises the immune system and makes the body more susceptible to (dis-ease) disease. Offense is the enemy's weapon of mass destruction used to root un-forgiveness, bitterness and soulful (mind, will and emotions) wounds.

Releasing those that have wounded us, forgiveness, allows the power of the Father to heal us physically, emotionally and spiritually. Some offenses are deeply rooted and difficult to let go of, which is why our Helper, (the Holy Spirit) has been sent to lead and guide us into that place of forgiveness.

You may not feel the release, but continue in faith, confessing your forgiveness of others as well as yourself and your emotions will catch up. Forgiveness is an act that we must choose to walk in. Confess over and over I CHOOSE (the surrendering of "my" will to the Heavenly Father's will) to forgive. Feed on the word of God to water that seed as you work out daily, the process of forgiveness and watch the power of the word manifest in your life and in the lives of others. Signs, wonders and miracles follow the word.

Have you ever wondered why God requires that we pray for our enemies, those who despitefully use us? Because offense (which will come) hardens the heart, which opens the door to un-forgiveness making the heart cold. God cannot work through a contaminated harden heart – it will reject Him. But prayer has the supernatural ability to make tender even the most harden heart. As you pray for those who offend you, your heart is made tender before the Lord and un-forgiveness, which deafens your ear to the voice of God, cannot remain.

Prayer

Lord, I need You to heal me from the inside out. I ask that You come into my heart and reveal any un-forgiveness that may have taken residency in me, toward others or myself and remove it from me. Go deep into the unconscious realm of my soul and reveal any undetected or un-confessed un-forgiveness that may be lying dormant in my heart. Forgive me Lord for walking in un-forgiveness and I ask You to take back any ground I may have given up to the enemy as a result. I bind all un-forgiveness and say yes to the emotional healing of my soul. I receive Your forgiveness and ask You to empower me to now pour out that very forgiveness to those who have hurt or offended me. Lord GOD, I ask forgiveness of any offense I may have inflicted on others and I pray that un-forgiveness has no place in their soul. Search my heart and know me and if there be any wicked way in me, cleanse me of all unrighteousness. I CHOOSE to forgive _____ and ask You to bless them. I CHOOSE to forgive myself that shame; guilt and condemnation will have no place in my life. Lord, help me to humbly surrender my will to You and do Your will which is to forgive. Thank You Father, for Your promise to be near to the brokenhearted. As I release forgiveness, You are flooding me with Your healing power that not only heals my soul, but my body as well. I serve satan notice that his wicked trap to root un-forgiveness in my heart through offenses, wounds, hurts and anger, have no power or authority to become a foothold or stumbling block in my path. For greater is He that is in me than the spirit of un-forgiveness. I CHOOSE to live a life of forgiveness and receive my healing. In Jesus name I confidently pray.

A Heart That Chases After You

Acts 13:22 – I have found David son of Jesse, a man after My own heart; he will do everything I want him to do.

Colossians 3:15 – And let the peace (soul harmony which comes) from Christ rule (act as umpire continually) in your hearts (deciding and settling with finality all questions that arise in your minds, in that peaceful state) to which as (members of Christ's) one body you were also called to live. And be thankful (appreciative), giving praise to God always.

Psalm 24:3-4 – Who shall go up into the mountain of the Lord? Or who shall stand in His Holy Place? He who has clean hands and a pure heart...

Psalm 108:1 – O God, my heart is fixed (steadfast, in the confidence of faith), I will sing, yes, I will sing praises, even with my glory (all the faculties and powers of one created in Your image)!

Psalm 86:12-13 – I will confess and praise You, O Lord my God, with my whole (united) heart; and I will glorify Your name forevermore. For great is Your mercy and loving-kindness toward me; and You have delivered me from the depths of Sheol (from the exceeding depths of affliction).

Joel 2:12 – Therefore, turn to me and keep on coming to Me with all your heart, with fasting, with weeping, and with mourning (until every hindrance is removed and the broken fellowship is restored).

Luke 10:27 – You must love the Lord your God with all your heart and with all your soul and with all your strength and with all your mind and your neighbor as yourself.

Psalm 119:32-34 – I will (not merely walk, but) run the way of Your commandments, when You give me a heart that is willing. Teach me, O Lord, the way of Your statutes and I will keep it to the end (steadfastly). Give me understanding, (in my heart) that I may keep Your law; yes, I will observe it with my whole heart.

Ezekiel 11:19 – And I will give them one heart (a new heart) and I will put a new spirit within them; and I will take the stony (unnaturally hardened) heart out of their flesh and will give them a heart of flesh (sensitive and responsive to the touch of God).

2 Chronicles 19:3 – But there are good things found in you… you have set your heart to seek God (with all your soul's desire).

Jeremiah 29:13 – Then you will seek Me, inquire for, and require Me (as a vital necessity) and find Me when you search for Me with all your heart.

Proverbs 4:23 – Keep and guard your heart with all vigilance and above all that you guard, for out of it flow the springs of life.

The condition of the heart determines whether a person can live fully, without limitations, or even sustain life at all. Just as in the natural body, the heart determines the vitality of your spiritual life as well. A heart that chases after God longs for His direction, recognizes His sovereignty and believes in His power. It is a heart that is surrendered to Him, allowing Him to deposit His heart into us so we may be His people and He may be our God.

In the same manner that you received salvation, you must receive one's healing. It is with the "heart" that you believe onto salvation. And it is with the "heart" that you must believe in God's healing power. Your heart must be fixed on His word that promises healing in our spirit, as well as our bodies. The word of God says the natural un-renewed heart is wicked (untrustworthy, deceitful) so who can know it. He promised to take away that heart, which is a heart that cannot believe, and give us His heart, that is ready to believe. When we give our hearts to God and allow Him to circumcise (cut away through His love and His word) everything that would hinder us from believing such as shame, bitterness, guilt, un-forgiveness, fear, offense, worry, unworthiness or doubt, then can we truly believe and receive. It is the cleansing power of His word that renews the heart and turns it to the Father, giving you the passion to chase after Him with all your might. Our Lord longs for His heart and your heart to beat to the same rhythm, to be one with Him, which requires the surrendering of all your heart. Surrender the fear that tries to grip your heart and compromise your faith, surrender the hurts that in a self- protective attempt you have closed your heart to receiving, and surrender the doubt that comes to challenge your belief. Let our Father create in you a new heart that is pliable for the Master's use and able to believe and receive His promise of healing.

Prayer

Heavenly Father thank You for Your incorruptible, uncompromising word that is able to turn the hearts of kings, mend the hearts of the hurting and bring healing to Your people. Give me Lord, the desires of my heart by taking away my selfish desires, and giving me Your desires. Search me and circumcise anything that may compete for Your place in my heart. Remove from me those things that do not please You or anything that refuses to chase after You. Purify me with hyssop and I shall be clean, wash me and I shall be whiter than snow (Psalm 51:7). Then shall I seek You with all my soul's desire. For when I seek You, inquire of You and yes require of You as my vital necessity I will find You (Jeremiah 29:13). As I seek You with all my heart, You release me from all captivity. I thank You Father for giving me a heart that is willing to seek You, to serve You, and to trust You with all that I am. For in You, I live and move and have my being (Acts 17:28). Thank You Father, Amen.

❧ ✳✳ ☙

You Hear My Prayers

Psalm 4:1 – Answer me when I call, O God of my righteousness (uprightness, justice, and right standing with You)! You have freed me when I was hemmed in and enlarged me when I was in distress; have mercy upon me and hear my prayer.

Exodus 22:27 – When he cries to Me I will hear, for I am gracious and merciful.

Jeremiah 29:12 – Then you will call upon Me and you will come and pray to Me and I will hear and heed you.

Psalm 3:4 – With my voice I cry to the Lord and He hears and answers me out of His holy hill.

Psalm 116:1-2 – I love the Lord, because He has heard (and now hears) my voice and my supplications. Because He has inclined His ear to me, therefore will I call upon Him as long as I live.

Proverbs 15:29 – The Lord is far from the wicked, but He hears the prayer of the (consistently) righteous (the upright, in right standing with Him).

Galatians 4:6 – And because you (really) are (His) sons, God has sent the (Holy) Spirit of His Son into our hearts, crying, Abba (Father)! Father!

God, our Father, has promised to hear those in right standing in Him. Uprightness is established in the heart of those who surrender to Him. His righteousness is a gift. We cannot earn it through our own works or doings. For our righteousness (self-centered efforts), which are our meager attempts to be right, are works of the flesh, but His righteousness which He freely gives, is of His Spirit. It's not what we do right that makes us righteous, but it's our surrendering to Him and receiving His righteousness that Christ made available to us through His sacrifice on the cross.

Our Father hears our prayers, cries, and supplications. He answers the voice of His children. We commune with God through prayer and He longs to commune with us. He is Abba Father "the Father" who hears and answers. We are His children who trust and listen for His small, still voice to speak to our hearts.

Prayer
Father I come to You with a heart of eager anticipation, knowing You are my God who hears and answers my prayers. Thank You for being my Abba Father who cares for me and has made me Your righteousness through Christ Jesus. I will confidently present my prayers and petitions to You, for I trust and believe that Your ear is turned to my every need. You are the Lord GOD that healeth me, that hears my cry and answers, for You are gracious and merciful. Help me Lord to take all my concerns, fears, doubts and worries to You in prayer with confidence that You hear me. In Jesus name I pray.

$\mathcal{N}$ever Stop Believing and Trusting in Him

Matthew 21:22 – And whatever you ask for in prayer, having faith and believing, you will receive.

John 12:44 – But Jesus loudly declared, the one who believes in Me does not (only) believe in and trust in and rely on Me, but (believing in Me he believes) in Him who sent Me.

Psalm 62:5-6 – My soul, wait only upon God and silently submit to Him, for hope and expectation are from Him. He only is my Rock and my Salvation; He is my Defense and my Fortress, I shall not be moved.

James 2:23 – And the Scripture was fulfilled that says, Abraham believed in (adhered to, trusted in, and relied on) God, and this was accounted to him as righteousness (as conformity to God's will in thought and deed) and he was called God's friend.

Psalm 27:13 – What would have become of me had I not believed that I would see the Lord's goodness in the land of the living?

John 2:22 – When therefore He had risen from the dead, His disciples remembered that He said this. And so they believed and trusted and relied on the Scripture and the word (message) Jesus had spoken.

Mark 11:24-25 – For this reason, I am telling you, whatever you ask for in prayer, believe (trust and be confident) that it is granted to you and you will (get it). And whenever you stand praying, if you have anything against anyone, forgive him and let it drop (leave it, let it go) in order that your

Father Who is in heaven may also forgive you your (own) failings and shortcomings and let them drop.

1 John 3:23 – And this is His order (His command, His injunction) that we should believe in (put our faith and trust in and adhere to and rely on) the name of His Son Jesus Christ (the Messiah) and that we should love one another, just as He has commanded us.

Hebrews 11:1 – (KJV) – Now faith is the substance of things hoped for the evidence of things not seen.

Mark 2:5 – And when Jesus saw their faith (their confidence in God through Him), He said to the paralyzed man, son, your sins are forgiven (you) and put away (that is, the penalty is remitted, the sense of guilt removed, and you are made upright and in right standing with God).

The word, *believe* means to have faith in, to entrust and commit to with confidence and putting your trust in. It means to accept as true, genuine or real and to be permanent, certain and steadfast in. *Trust* means to be confident and sure, to have hope and take refuge in, and to be secure and assured of. Faith is believing, trusting and remaining loyal to the word of the Lord GOD our Father. He requires that we walk by faith and not by sight and commands that we believe in and trust on the matchless name of Jesus.

Only through the gift of our Lord's salvation, a personal relationship with Christ Jesus and the ever empowering word of God, can we have the faith to believe that which we cannot see and remain in allegiance to a God we cannot touch. Now faith is the assurance (the confirmation, the title deed) of those things (we) hope for, being the proof of things (we) do not see and the conviction of their reality (faith perceiving as real fact what is not revealed to the senses) (Hebrews 11:1). Faith pleases God. Without faith, it is impossible to please and be satisfactory to Him. For whoever would come near to God must (necessarily) believe that God exists and that He is the Rewarder of those who earnestly and diligently seek Him (Hebrews 11:6).

Prayer

Lord I believe in You and now ask that You help me to be faithful (loyal) to what I believe. Help me to believe in that which I cannot see and to trust what I cannot comprehend through my natural mind. Give me the mind of Christ that I may confidently find my place of refuge in You. When I do not understand, I choose to trust You, when I cannot see what I have hoped in, I choose to believe in You. You have required of us to believe in You and I pray for an immovable spirit of obedience to Your command. In 1 Peter 2:7, Your word refers to our believing as preciousness and it is my desire to be held precious in Your sight. Thank You Lord for the privilege granted to us for Christ's sake, to believe in, adhere to, rely on and trust in You (Philippians 1:29). In Jesus name. Amen.

Expect Your Healing

1 Peter 2:24 – He personally bore our sins in His (own) body on the tree (as on an altar and offered Himself on it), that we might die (cease to exist) to sin and live to righteousness. By His wounds (stripes) you have been healed.

Isaiah 53:5 – But He was wounded for our transgressions, He was bruised for our guilt and iniquities; the chastisement (needful to obtain) of our peace and well-being for us was upon Him, and with the stripes (that wounded) Him we are healed and made whole.

Psalm 25:21 – Let integrity and uprightness preserve me, for I wait for and expect You.

Isaiah 40:31 – But those who wait for the Lord (who expect, look for, and hope in Him) shall change and renew their strength and power; they shall lift their wings and mount up (close to God) as eagles (mount up to the sun); they shall run and not get weary, they shall walk and not faint or become tired.

Psalm 25:5 – Guide me in Your truth and faithfulness and teach me, for You are the God of my salvation; for You (You only and altogether) do I wait (expectantly) all the day long.

Psalm 27:14 – Wait and hope for and expect the Lord; be brave and of good courage and let your heart be stout (brave and bold) and enduring. Yes, wait for and hope for and expect the Lord.

Psalm 25:3 – Yes, let none who trust and wait hopefully and look for You be put to shame or be disappointed...

Romans 8:25 – But if we hope for what is still unseen by us, we wait (anticipate) for it with patience and composure.

We are not trying to get our healing; we are the "Healed" shielding our health through the word of God and our relationship with Christ Jesus, from the curse of sickness and disease. Healing is the completed work done on the Cross of Christ.

We may not always get what we want, but we usually get that in which we have set our minds to expect. Just as your words shape your life; your expectations govern your experiences in this life. To expect means to think (rehearse in your mind; meditate on), suppose, await, consider as certain, anticipate, and watch for. You must "expect" healing because of who you are in Christ Jesus, you are the "Healed". Your mind must think on healing, your words must speak and confess healing, your heart must be set on healing and your expectation must be "I am healed."

The power to walk in divine health does not rest in whether you earned it or if the things you do qualify you to be a recipient. It rest solely in the ultimate sacrifice of love made on our behalf by Christ, through His crucifixion, (becoming our substitutionary sacrifice), His resurrection, and God's unconditional love for us, absolutely nothing else. Jesus paid such an immense, painstaking, incomprehensible price for us that it cannot even be grasped in our natural mind.

Now receive His gift of healing as yours and expect the manifestation by faith, because "now" (today, at this moment, before you can see it) faith is the substance of things hoped for and the evidence of things not seen (Hebrews 11:1). Believe it, receive it, and be it.

Prayer

I come before You Lord, humbled by the "Act of Love," Jesus offered on the Cross that has made healing available to me. I believe He died for me, and my sins are forgiven. He rose from the dead that I may walk in the total victory of His sacrifice through salvation which includes my healing. He ascended into heaven, now seated at the right hand of the Father making intercession for me. Not only do I believe, but

I expect the manifestation of that in which I believe. Thank You for giving your children a measure of faith that empowers me to call those things that are not as though they were. I call myself "The Healed" and expect the fruit of my lips and the certainty of my expectation to come forth. Heavenly Father, I ask that You continue to renew my thinking and my expectations as I meditate and study Your word. I pray that the eyes of my understanding be enlightened and that I may grow in the knowledge of everything that Your salvation affords me. I confidently pray in Jesus name.

Trust In The Lord

Proverbs 3:5-6 – Lean on, trust in, and be confident in the Lord with all your heart and mind and do not rely on your own insight or understanding. In all your ways know, recognize, and acknowledge Him, and He will direct and make straight and plain your path.

Psalm 5:11 – But let all those who take refuge and put their trust in You rejoice; let them ever sing and shout for joy, because You make a covering over them and defend them; let those also who love Your name be joyful in You and be in high spirits.

Psalm 18:2 – The Lord is my Rock, my Fortress, and my Deliverer; my God, my keen and firm Strength in Whom I will trust and take refuge, my Shield, and the horn of my salvation, my High Tower.

Nahum 1:7 – The Lord is good, a Strength and Stronghold in the day of trouble; He knows (recognizes, has knowledge of, and understands) those who take refuge and trust in Him.

Psalm 16:8-10 – I have set the Lord continually before me; because He is at my right hand, I shall not be moved. Therefore my heart is glad and my glory (my inner self) rejoices; my body too shall rest and confidently dwell in safety.

Psalm 46:10 – Let be and be still and know (recognize and understand) that I am God.

Isaiah 12:2 – Behold, God my salvation! I will trust and not be afraid, for the Lord God is my strength and song; yes, He has become my salvation.

Trust is our conscience ability to rely on, believe in and depend on with confidence, the unexplainable endless power of the Almighty to do exactly what He has promised and to answer all things. It's to know that you know that you know that God is real and well able to complete, heal and rescue us from every struggle. Trust is learning to rest and be assured that God is the great "I AM" ready and willing to meet our needs. It develops and grows every time we are willing to step out on faith and believe that God will do what He said He will do. It is strengthened when we choose to believe that which we cannot yet see. Trust is established every time we allow God to show Himself strong through our weaknesses. It is difficult to trust in a God you cannot see or a promise you cannot touch in the natural mind. But the word of God renews (makes new spiritually) our mind and enables us to see and receive by faith that which the natural mind cannot comprehend. To trust requires you to turn away from your own abilities and lean onto His.

Prayer
Heavenly Father I will trust in You with all my heart and not lean onto my own understanding (Proverbs 3:5). In times of uncertainty, I will seek Your face and listen for Your voice

46

that I may confidently rely on and rest in You. You are the great "I AM". You are my Great Physician, my Refuge, my Safety, my Healer, and my Lord. I bind every spirit of distrust that may have taken root in my heart as a result of betrayal or broken promises of man. For You are not a man that You would lie, but You are my Abba Father whose promises never return back void (Isaiah 55:11; Num. 23:19). Remove from me every self-protective stance that refuses to rely on You out of fear. Take from me the spirit of pride that only desires to depend on its own abilities. I will trust You Lord with all my soul, my heart, my mind and my might that I may be the vessel that You can show Yourself strong in. Yes Lord, I trust in the completed work of Calvary that has healed my body and freed my soul. I pray in the authority of Jesus name.

Binding the Spirit of Fear

2 Timothy 1:7 – For God did not give us a spirit of fear (timidity), but He has given us a spirit of power and of love and of calm and well-balanced mind and discipline and self-control.

Philippians 4:6 – Do not fret or have any anxiety about anything, but in every circumstance and in everything, by prayer and petition, with thanksgiving, continue to make your request known to God. And God's peace… which transcends all understanding shall garrison and mount guard over your heart and mind in Christ Jesus.

Exodus 14:13-14 – …Fear not; stand still (firm, confident, undismayed) and see the salvation of the Lord which He will work for you today. The Lord will fight for you and you shall hold your peace and remain at rest.

47

1 John 4:18-19 (KJV) – There is no fear in love; but perfect love casteth out all fear; because fear hath torment. He that feareth is not (yet) made perfect in love. We love Him, because He first loved us.

Hebrews 10:38 – But the just shall live by faith and if he draws back and shrinks in fear, My soul has no delight or pleasure in him.

Fear compromises your ability to believe and hinders you from walking by faith. It is the result of uncertainties and the lack of trust (safety) in those uncertain times. It produces worry, anxiety, fret, dread and stress. Fear brings torment and that is not of God, but of the enemy (1 John 4:18). The only fear we can afford to have is the reverential fear (honor, love and respect) for the Lord God. If fear is permitted to remain in your thoughts, emotions and words, it will plant a spirit of doubt and unbelief that will battle against the truth of the word of God that promises your healing. Fear must be directly and immediately defeated through faith which God has given all of us. Faith exposes fear for what it really is – a contrary lie of the enemy intended to paralyze the people of God by settling unbelief and doubt in our spirits. But faith which is the substance of things hoped for and the evidence of things not seen; stands and speaks those things that are not as though they were through faith filled eyes. The word of God is the greatest weapon against fear, because it builds your faith and faith comes by hearing and hearing by the word of God. Take the word of God and use it to overcome fear each time it tries to grip your heart (Hebrews 11:1; Romans 10:17).

Prayer
Lord thank You for not giving me a spirit of fear, but of power, love and a sound mind (2 Timothy 1:7). Teach me Father,

how to walk daily in this revelation. Reveal any areas of my life where negativity and unbelief have open doors to the spirit of fear. Cover me with Your love and open my heart to receive and understand, so Your love may be perfected in me. I will place Your word in my heart to set guard against the spirit of fear, that it may not be able to grip my heart and challenge my faith. Surround me Lord with people of great faith that are encouragers, and speak life, are unwavering and uplifting, for two are better than one and if one falls the other will lift him up (2 Timothy 1:7; Ecclesiastes 4:10). In Jesus name I fearlessly pray.

꠱∗∗꠲

Take Courage

Matthew 9:21-22 – For she kept saying to herself, if I only touch His garment I shall be restored to health. Jesus turned around and seeing her, He said Take courage daughter! Your faith has made you well. And at once the woman was restored to health.

Nehemiah 4:14 – … Do not be afraid of the enemy (earnestly) remember the Lord and imprint Him (on your minds) great and terrible and take from Him courage to fight…

Psalm 31:24 – Be strong and let your heart take courage, all you that wait for and hope for and expect the Lord!

Joshua 1:9 – Be strong, vigorous, and very courageous. Be not afraid, neither be dismayed, for the Lord your God is with you wherever you go.

Matthew 9:2 – …when Jesus saw their faith, He said…Take courage, your sins are forgiven and the penalty remitted.

Psalm 18:2 – The Lord is my Rock, my Fortress, and my Deliverer; my God, my keen and firm Strength in whom I will trust and take refuge, my Shield and the Horn of my salvation, my High Tower.

2 Corinthians 7:4 – I have great boldness and free and fearless confidence and cheerful courage toward you…

Joshua 10:25 – …Fear not nor be dismayed; be strong and of good courage.

Ezra 10:4 – Be strong and brave and do it.

Webster's dictionary defines *courage* as the mental or moral strength to venture, persevere, and withstand danger, fear, or difficulty. *Take* is defined as the ability to get possession, power or control of. God's word instructs us to take (gain possession of) courage. The mental strength to persevere and withstand fear and difficulty, while standing in faith and believing on His promise. The trials that are before us do not mitigate nor compromise this promise. If He requires it of you then He has already deposited it in you. Fear and uncertainty may come, but do it anyway. Believe and stand, refusing to be moved, until you see the manifestation. Actively believe by taking courage from the Lord GOD and going forward in the healing He promised. Regardless of what it may look like, sound like or feel like, remain steadfast. It will take courage! But the Lord has made available in Himself, the courage needed to fight and stand firm. Yes, fear will come, doubt will knock and unbelief will try to find place in your heart, but be strong and of good courage, for the Lord shall strengthen you.

Prayer
Heavenly Father, I come and take courage from You that I

may stand firm and immovable during this time of trouble. I will not be afraid, but I will seek Your direction, resting assured that You are with me wherever I go. I will wait for, hope for and expect You Lord to manifest through Your word in my life. I am strong and courageous and my heart takes courage. That courage needed to persevere and withstand the attacks of the enemy against my body, my mind and my soul. I am not without hope and actively believe that my God is able to do exceedingly, abundantly above and beyond all I can ask or think, according to the power that worketh in me and I take courage in it (Ephesians 3:20 – KJV). I pray in the powerful name of Jesus.

❧ ** ❧

Cast Your Cares

1 Peter 5:7 – Casting the whole of your care, (all your anxieties and all your worries, all your concerns once and for all) on Him for He cares for you affectionately and cares about you watchfully.

Ezekiel 18:31 – Cast away from you all your transgressions by which you have transgressed against Me, and make you a new mind and heart and a new spirit.

Matthew 11:28-30 – (KJV) – Come onto Me all ye that labour and are heavy laden and I will give you rest. Take My yoke (cast your yoke, burden, cares onto Me and take up Mine) upon you and learn of Me; for I Am meek and lowly in heart and ye shall find rest unto your souls. For My yoke is easy and My burden is light.

Psalm 138:8 – The Lord will perfect that which concerns me; Your mercy and loving-kindness, O Lord, endure forever.

51

Casting your cares and leaving them with God is a daily commitment. It requires a level of faith that can only develop through a constant connection to the One in which you will release it to. You would think that we would have no problem "releasing" concerns or worries and simply letting them go, but we do. To release one's cares requires trust and confidence that the One you are releasing it to will resolve and take care of them. As mentioned previously, fear, anxiety and a self-protective stance will hinder your ability to trust. Many times you may fear whether you can trust God to take care of your every need. Sometimes you may trust that God can do it, but wonder, will He do it for me. You must come to the revelation, which results from a personal relationship with God through His word that God "cares" for you. He is more than able to fulfill His every promise to you including healing. In Ezekiel 18:31, God promises to give you a new mind, a new heart and a new spirit. Meditate on this word, think on it, and ponder it, so that God will have a place to deposit the new mind and heart. Being able to cast is a matter of being able to trust. Once you cast it onto God, into His more than capable hands, then you must allow your trust to go to work to tie that thing to the altar you casted it upon and secure it there. Your trust will rise up and victoriously defeat doubt, fear, worry and anxiety.

Trust is built through knowing, recognizing, identifying and becoming acquitted with the One in Whom you place that trust. God has asked you to cast, which means to throw violently in another direction, your cares (fears, worries, stressors, unbelief, doubt…) onto Him. To throw something it requires the "releasing" (to give up and let go) of that thing. You must be willing to let go and release in order to accept and receive. Cast (throw forcefully) your cares upon the Lord so you will be able and ready to receive His promises.

Prayer

Lord, my heart has been burdened with so many emotions and cares. I come to You and ask for You to direct my path and enable me to cast all my fears, concerns and cares onto You and leave them in Your trustworthy hands. Remind me Lord of Your great love for me and Your endless desire to take care of my concerns. Teach me how to confidently cast my cares onto You and to trust in You with all my heart without wavering. As I grow in Your word, my ability to trust and release will increase. I thank You for patiently leading me into a relationship of trust in You. This relationship empowers me to let go and release so that I may accept and receive all that You have for me including healing in my body, my heart and my soul (mind, will and emotions). Through the powerful name of Jesus I pray.

The Joy Of The Lord Is My Strength

Nehemiah 8:10 – And be not grieved and depressed, for the joy of the Lord is your strength and stronghold.

Psalm 13:5 – But I have trusted, leaned on and been confident in Your mercy and loving-kindness; my heart shall rejoice and be in high spirits in Your salvation.

Psalm 16:11 – You will show me the path of life; in Your presence is fullness of joy, at Your right hand there are pleasures forevermore.

Acts 2:28 –You have made known to me the ways of life; You will enrapture me (diffusing my soul with joy) with and in Your Presence.

Psalm 126:5 – They who sow in tears shall reap in joy and singing.

Jeremiah 33:11 – There shall be heard again the voice of joy and the voice of gladness…give thanks to the Lord of host, for the Lord is good; for His mercy and kindness and steadfast love endure forever.

Job 8:21 – He will yet fill your mouth with laughter and your lips with joyful shouting.

Proverbs 17:22 – A happy heart is good medicine and a cheerful mind works healing.

Proverbs 15:13 – A glad heart makes a cheerful countenance.

Jeremiah 15:16 –…Your words were to me a joy and the rejoicing of my heart, for I am called by Your name.

The joy of the Lord is our place of strength, assurance, peace and rejoicing. In the midst of difficult, uncertain times, it may appear impossible to find joy in anything. However, the joy of the Lord is not conditioned according to your circumstance, but according to your relationship with the Lord GOD who is able to do what is seemingly impossible for man. The Lord's joy is found in His Presence and is unexplainable and unspeakable. It brings a peace that surpasses our natural human understanding. We can't earn it, nor grasp it in our limited emotions. It is the supernatural presence of the Lord that springs forth from the well of our trust in Him and overshadows every situation that comes to challenge our belief. The joy of the Lord is a place of safety and security that only our Abba Father can provide. Our Lord finds joy in our believing in His word, and our faith in His promises which pleases Him without limits. Joy from above brings healing to every area of your life and peace to your mind.

A cheerful heart, which produces a peaceful mind, readily and eagerly waits, without fret, on the Lord and openly, with confidence, receives and holds fast His promises. In that peaceful wait, His joy imparts His strength which is made strong in our weakness (2 Corinthians 12:9). This type of joy will keep you steadfast and immovable in circumstances that otherwise would bring you to hopelessness and despair. The joy of the Lord is found in His Presence, in His word, in the place of worship, in the praises of His people, and in intimate fellowship with the Father who refuses to ever leave you.

Prayer

I declare that the joy of the Lord is truly my strength and my source of endurance. It is my godly stronghold in times of trouble and my peace in the face of turmoil. Yes, Lord Your joy keeps me and empowers me to remain steadfast and settled when my emotions are unsettled. Your word says that a cheerful heart that produces laughter is like a medicine (Proverbs 17:22), bringing forth healing and restoration to the mind and body. Therefore, I declare that I walk in the gift of laughter and I am anointed with the oil of joy. I walk in Your "Joy" Father that surpasses my understanding and causes the storms in my life to be quieted. I stand in joyful confidence that I will reap joy and singing for the tears I have sown. I pray in the power of Jesus name. Amen.

I Am An Overcomer

John 16:33 – For I have overcome the world (I have deprived it of power to harm you and have conquered it for you).

1 John 5:4 – For whatsoever is born of God overcometh the world; and this is the victory that overcometh the world, even our faith.

Revelation 12:11 – And they overcame by the blood of the Lamb and by the word of their testimony…

2 Corinthians 2:14 (KJV) – Now thanks be unto God, Who always causeth us to triumph in Christ.

Romans 8:37 – Yet amid all these things we are more than conquerors and gain a surpassing victory through Him Who loved us.

We overcome, defeat, prevail, subdue and triumph over the enemy by the shed blood of Christ on the cross. The words that proceed from our mouth, testify to the supernatural work accomplished by our Lord's love-filled sacrifice. We overcome cancer and every disease, virus and infirmity in Christ Jesus. Victory is yours if you surrender and lose yourself in Christ in the secret place of the Most High – His Presence. God empowers us and leads us through the Holy Spirit into victory over every trial, every test and every tribulation. Absolutely no weapon formed against us has the power to overtake us, but will only prove to strengthen, secure, establish and fortify us in Christ Jesus.

Prayer
Thank You Lord for Your world overcoming faith that resides on the inside of me empowering me to overcome every challenge. I am an overcomer and I overcome by the blood of the Lamb, that supreme sacrifice of the Lord Jesus Christ and the word of my testimony that stands and says – I Am Healed (Revelation 12:11). I am victorious in every battle because You always cause me to triumph in Christ (2 Corinthians 2:14

- KJV). I am an overcomer, a champion in Christ, and more than a conqueror, working out, triumphantly, my salvation, my healing, and my victory daily. I am strengthened by Your glorious power and validated through the redemptive blood of Jesus that has made me whole, cleansed, and healed. I can do all things through Christ who strengthened me (Philippians 4:13 - KJV). In Jesus name I confidently pray.

$\mathcal{K}$now He Will Never Leave You Nor Forsake You

Joshua 1:9 – Be not afraid, neither be dismayed, for the Lord your God is with you wherever you go.

John 14:18 (KJV) – I will not leave you comfortless; I will come to you.

John 14:27 – Do not let your hearts be troubled, neither let them be afraid.

1 Samuel 12:22 – The Lord will not forsake His people for His great Name's sake, for it has pleased Him to make you a people for Himself.

Psalm 46:1 – GOD is our Refuge and Strength (mighty and impenetrable to temptation) a very present and well-proved help in time of trouble.

1 Chronicles 28:20 – Fear not, be not dismayed, for the Lord, my God, is with you.

We serve a God who is both faithful and just. His faithfulness is not compromised by our unfaithfulness. He has promised to never forsake us and He cannot forsake His own word. In times of struggle, the blessed assurance that God is near brings a comfort that soothes even the darkest hour. God does not waver in His commitment to His people nor withhold His love that shelters you in the storm. Regardless of where you are, He is standing by.

Prayer
Father, help me to know that You are near. You are my place of refuge and my strength, my everlasting Father and healer

of all disease. Knowing You are close Lord is the security I need to remain stable and rooted. Thank You for never leaving or forsaking me. When I have no place to turn or a shoulder to cry upon, I rest assured that You are here. Keep me close Lord, that I may walk through the waters and not be overtaken and that I may walk through the fire and not be consumed. (Isaiah 43:2) In You Lord and You alone, do I place my trust. In Jesus name I pray.

>***<

When I'm Weary

Isaiah 40:28-29 – The everlasting God, the Lord, the Creator of the ends of the earth, does not faint or grow weary…He gives power to the faint and weary and to him who has no might He increases strength.

Isaiah 40:31 – But those who wait for the Lord (who expect, look for and hope in Him) shall change and renew their strength and power; they lift their wings and mount up (close to God) as eagles; they shall run and not be weary, they shall walk and not faint or become tired.

Matthew 11:28-29 – Come to Me, all you who labor and are heavy-laden and overburdened and I will cause you to rest.

Psalm 23:2 (KJV) – He restoreth my soul, He leadeth me in the paths of righteousness for His name's sake.

Proverbs 17:22 – A happy heart is good medicine and a cheerful mind works healing…

Psalm 103:2 – Bless the LORD, O my soul, and forget not all His benefits; who forgives all your iniquities, Who heals all your disease…

James 5:15 – And the prayer (that is) of faith will save him who is sick and the Lord will restore him; and if he has committed sins, he will be forgiven.

2 Thessalonians 3:13 – ...Do not become weary or lose heart in doing right but continue in well-doing without weakening.

Weariness is to be completely exhausted and in need of a place of rest and restoration. The Lord God will renew your strength and lift burdens, for He is the "Burden Lifter" and the "Lifter of Your Head". God never intended for you to carry the burdens that are weighing you down. He requires you to cast your cares and depend on Him. Allow God to be your "Burden Lifter" and release the heavy weights that can so easily cause you to stumble and be weakened.

Prayer
Lord, I ask You to reveal to me every weight, burden and yoke that has so easily beset me and cause me to lose focus (Hebrews 12:1). I stand on Your word that promises to renew my strength like the eagle and to restore my soul. I speak and declare total restoration of my body, my mind, my family, my finances and my walk with You.

I am so thankful that You do not faint or grow weary. I confess that I will not grow weary in well doing, but You will renew my strength and enable me to run this race with joy. I bind and command to leave, every negative thought that would give place to depression and oppression. I have been redeemed from the curse of sickness and resist the enemy. I choose to think on things that are good, pure, pleasing and of good report (Philippians. 4:8) which will war against the spirit of weariness. Father, reveal to me any areas of my life that I am pushing myself too hard and need a time of rest and communion with Your word. I pray in the strength of Jesus name. Amen.

Breaking Generational Curses

Exodus 20:5-6 – Thou shall not bow down thyself to them, nor serve them, for I the Lord thy God am a jealous God, visiting the iniquity of the fathers upon the children unto the third and fourth generation of them that hate Me; But showing mercy and steadfast love unto a thousand generations of those who love Me, and keep My commandments.

Deuteronomy 5:10 – And (the Lord) showing mercy and steadfast love to thousands and to a thousand generations of those who love Me and keep My commandments.

John 14:15 – If you love Me, keep My commandments.

Isaiah 41:4 – Who has prepared and done this, calling forth and guides the destinies of the generations from the beginning? I, the Lord –the first (existing before history began) and with the last (an ever-present, unchanging God) –I am He.

John 8:36 – Who the Son sets free is free indeed.

Proverbs 26:2 (KJV) – As the bird by wandering, as the swallow by flying, so a curse causeless (without a cause) shall not come.

Ezekiel 18:14 – If, however he begets a son who sees all the sins which his father has done, and considers but does not do likewise…but has executed My judgments and walked in My statutes. He shall not die for the iniquity of his father; he shall surely live.

Bad habits, illnesses, mind sets and behaviors can unknowingly be passed down from one generation to the next, opening the door for a curse to transfer. It passes down from generation to generation through our blood line and is often mistakenly accepted as a part of our heritage. But we are new creations in Christ and have been given a new heritage in Christ Jesus. Our new blood line has redeemed us from the curse. However, we must know how to walk in the freedom Christ paid such a heavy price for. Breaking generational curses requires our minds to be renewed and set on the blessing God has given us and not the curse that His blood eradicated (pulled up from the roots). You must first surrender and submit your life to God, identify the curse and renounce it (resist and refuse to live according to its dictates). Then you must change your mind set towards it, the habits that support it and the words that empower it. Finally, proclaim and receive the generational blessings God has given to those who love and fear (reverence) Him.

Prayer

I come in the power of the Greater One that lives on the inside of me and renounce, nullify and eradicate every generational curse that has presumptuously remained in my blood line for forty generations back. I refuse to live under any curse because the Son of God has made me free and who the Son sets free, is free indeed. Holy Spirit, search my thoughts, the motives of my heart and uproot anything that would give place for a curse to rest and rule. Father, reveal to me any habits, attitudes, behaviors, generational fears, generational anger or generational un-forgiveness that would open me up to a curse. I now speak generational blessing over my children and my children's children. They shall not walk under a curse and cancer shall not lord over their bodies. Help me Lord to teach them how to live a life of godliness and unwavering faithfulness. In Jesus name I boldly pray. Amen.

Resting In the Lord

Psalm 37:7 – Be still and rest in the Lord; wait for Him and patiently lean yourself upon Him…

Hebrews 4:9 (KJV) – There remaineth therefore a rest to the people of God. For he that entered into His (God's) rest, he also hath ceased from his own works, as God did from His.

Psalm 16:8-9 – I have set the Lord continually before me; because He is at my right hand, I shall not be moved. Therefore my heart is glad and my glory (my inner self) rejoices; my body too shall rest and confidently dwell in safety…

Psalm 131:1-2 – LORD, my heart is not haughty, nor my eyes lofty; neither do I exercise myself in matters too great or in things too wonderful (high) for me. Surely I have calmed and quieted my soul, like a child weaned with his mother, like a weaned child is my soul within me (ceased from fretting).

Job 19:25 – For I know that my Redeemer and Vindicator lives…

Just as God sent His presence with Moses and His rest, so shall He do with you as He leads you along your path (Exodus 33:14). God has made available a rest for those who believe in, trust in and lean on Him with confidence. Rest is necessary for healing to have its full reign in your body. You must have rest, God's undisturbed peace and freedom from anxieties, (which results from leaning on, trusting in and relying on God's promises) in your spirit, soul (mind, will and emotions) and body.

Prayer

Father You said there remains a rest for Your people (Hebrews 4:9). I take hold of that promise now. Teach me Lord, how to enter into this rest and dwell there. Help me to calm and quiet my soul that I may hear Your voice and find comfort. Yes, my Redeemer lives and I can find rest in Him. I commit to being still and knowing that You are the God that healeth me. Thank You Lord for Your rest, that brings peace to my mind, restoration to my body and ease to my soul. I pray in the name of Jesus.

Maintaining Your Healing

Proverbs 4:4 – Let your heart hold fast My words; keep may commandments and live.

Hosea 12:6 – Therefore return to your God! Hold fast to love and mercy, to righteousness and justice, and wait (expectantly) for your God continually!

Hebrews 4:14 – Inasmuch then as we have a great High Priest Who has ascended and passed through the heavens, Jesus the Son of God, let us hold fast our confession (of faith in Him).

Revelation 2:25-26 – Only hold fast to what you have until I come. And he who overcomes (is victorious) and who obeys My commands to the (very) end (doing the works that please Me), I will give him authority and power over the nations.

Job 19:25 – For I know my Redeemer and Vindicator lives and at last He (the Last One) will stand upon the earth.

James 5:16 (KJV) – The effectual fervent prayer of the righteous availeth much.

I Thessalonians 5:17 – Be unceasing in prayer (praying perseveringly); Thank (God) in everything (no matter what the circumstances may be, be thankful and give thanks), for this is the will of God for you (who are) in Christ Jesus (the Revealer and Mediator of that will).

James 4:7-8 (KJV) – Submit yourselves therefore to God. Resist the devil, and he will flee from you. Draw nigh to God, and He will draw nigh to you.

In the book of James, we are directed to do three very significant things that will keep us under the shadow of the Most High and in His protection. We are to submit, resist and stay close to Him. In doing so we position ourselves in His dwelling place, His presence, where there is safety, shelter, covering and protection. We must learn how to perpetually dwell in this secret "Place". We do this by submitting ourselves wholeheartedly to His will, resisting (withstanding and opposing) the temptation of the enemy and remaining close to Him through His word, fellowship with the body of Christ and a personal relationship with Him. It requires a daily development of your intimate bonding with Christ and the commitment to stay the course that has been set before you by placing all your trust in Him.

Prayer

As I run the race that has been set before me Lord, I have resolved in my soul that I will not turn back. I choose to trust in You with all my heart and to remain steadfast. I find my "safe place" in You and You alone. When the load weighs down on me, I will call upon You in whom I can confidently place my trust. I am "believing" (actively, currently and continuously) in You Father and I settle that belief into my soul daily through Your uncompromising word that sets watch over my healing. I receive from You now, all the gifts Your salvation has made available to me. Amen and Amen.

Prayer of Salvation

I would again like to invite you to give your life to God. If you do not know Jesus Christ as your personal Lord and Savior, or have turned from Him and are ready to return back to the Arms of the Father, our Healer, then open your heart and receive His Salvation through this prayer. Salvation is available to all and through His salvation are the promises of His word made accessible to His born again children. Make Him Lord GOD over your life that you may obtain all His promises by faith. His word simply says if you acknowledge and confess with your lips that Jesus is Lord and in your heart believe (adhere to, trust in, and rely on the truth) that God raised Him (Jesus Christ) from the dead; you will be saved (Roman 10:9).

Prayer for Salvation
Heavenly Father I come to You now, knowing that I have sinned and I am a sinner. I accept Your word that promises if I confess my sins that You are faithful and just to forgive me of sin and cleanse me from all unrighteousness. I believe in my heart that You sent Your Son to die for me and He rose from the grave so that I may have eternal life. I ask and receive Your forgiveness and choose today to turn away from sin. I accept You as Lord and Savior of my life. Fill me with Your Holy Spirit and teach me to love Your Word which guides and directs my steps. Help me Lord to work out my

salvation daily and to walk in the fullness of Your gift. I am a born again child of God and I thank You Lord. In Jesus name I faithfully pray.

If you have invited Jesus into your heart and received Him as your Lord and Savior then you are now a forgiven child of the Most High God and all His promises, including healing and divine health, are now available to you. You must walk out this salvation daily through His word and by joining a bible teaching church who believes in the life changing power of the blood of Jesus. It is vital that you place the word of God into your spirit daily by reading, studying, confessing and living it out in your life day by day. Begin meditating on the scriptures provided with each prayer in this book and watch God move like you never thought imaginable. With God all things are possible.

I receive Your Healing in every area of my life.
In Jesus Name I boldly pray and confidently confess
"I Am Healed"
Amen.

❧ ✲✲✲✲✲✲✲✲✲✲✲✲✲✲✲✲✲✲✲✲✲✲✲✲✲✲✲✲✲✲✲✲✲✲✲✲✲✲✲ ❧

Thank you for sharing the word of God with me through this book. God is truly your Healer and His love for you is endless. Keep His word hidden in your heart and it will war for you, comfort you and speak to you even in the darkest hours. Weeping may endure for the night but joy comes in the morning (Psalm 30:5). We do not have a High Priest who is unable to understand and sympathize and have a shared feeling with our weakness and infirmities… (Hebrews 4:15).

He knows where you are. He knows the fears that challenge your faith, the hurt that attempts to harden your heart and the sickness that tries to deny His promise. BUT GOD is more than able to deliver, heal and set free all that TRUST in Him. I commit to continuing to lift you up in prayer as you "Victoriously Overcome" all through Christ who strengthens you.

$\mathcal{A}$ppendix

Living the Word Out Loud

John 1:1 – (KJV) –   In the beginning was the Word, and the Word was with God, and the Word was God.

Everything you will need begins in the word of God. It is the key to building your relationship with Christ that sustains you in the battle, brings you out of the battle, maintains and keeps you after the battle and strengthens you for the next battle.

Hebrews 4:12 – (KJV) – The word of God is quick, and powerful, and sharper than any two-edged sword...

The word of God has the power and the ability to heal both the body and the soul.

Inundate your thoughts, your words, and your actions with the word of the Lord. Pray it, read it, study it, memorize it, think on it, speak it, and take it daily as a spiritual medicine that it may change not only your physical body but your entire life for eternity. **"Ask" God to give you a heart that is radically in love with His word** and keep asking until it is made manifested. For His word is a sword that attacks and destroys every fiery dart the enemy brings your way.

Scripture References
Spiritual Medicine for the Body and Soul
(Mind, Will and Emotions)

Prayer of Salvation

Exodus 14:13 – …Fear not, stand still, (firm, confident, undismayed) and see the salvation of the Lord which He will work for you today.

Exodus 15:2 – The Lord is my Strength and my Song, and He has become my Salvation; this is my God, and I will praise Him, my father's God, and I will exalt Him.

2 Samuel 22:3 – My God, My Rock, in Him will I take refuge; my Shield and the Horn of my salvation; my Stronghold and my Refuge, my Savior – You save me…

Psalm 3:8 – Salvation belongs to the Lord; May Your blessing be upon your people.

Psalm 80:3 – Restore us again, O God, and cause Your face to shine (in pleasure and approval on us) and we shall be saved!

Isaiah 38:20 – The Lord is ready to save (deliver) me…

The Power of God's Word

John 1:1 - In the beginning (before all time) was the Word (Christ) and the Word was with God, and the Word was God, Himself.

Hebrews 4:12 – For the Word that God speaks is alive and full of power (making it active, operative, energizing and effective); it is sharper than any two-edged sword, penetrating to the dividing line of the breath of life (soul) and (the immortal) spirit and of joints and marrow (of the deepest parts of our nature) exposing and sifting and analyzing and judging the very thoughts and purpose of the heart.

James 4:7-8 – Submit yourselves therefore to God. Resist the devil and he will flee from you. Draw nigh (close) to God and He will draw nigh (close) to you.

Ezekiel 11:19 – And I will give them one heart (a new heart) and I will put a new spirit within them and I will take the stony (unnaturally hardened) heart out of their flesh and will give them a heart of flesh sensitive and responsive to the touch of their God.

Psalm 16:11 – You will show me the path of life; in Your presence is fullness of joy, at Your right hand there are pleasures forevermore.

Colossians 3:16 – Let the word (spoken by) Christ (the Messiah) have its home (in your hearts and minds) and dwell in you in (all its) richness, as you teach and admonish and train one another on all insight and intelligence and wisdom (in spiritual things and as you sing) psalms and hymns and spiritual songs, making melody to God with (His) grace in your hearts.

*P*ray Your Way Through and Praise Your Way To

James 5:13-15 – Is anyone among you afflicted? He should pray. Is anyone glad at heart? He should sing praise (to God). Is anyone among you sick? He should call the church elders (the spiritual guides). And they should pray over him, anointing him with oil in the Lord's name. And the prayer of faith will save him, who is sick, and the Lord will restore him; and if he has committed sins, he will be forgiven.

James 5:16 – Confess to one another therefore your faults (your slips, your false steps, your offenses, your sins) and pray for one another, that you may be healed and restored (to the spiritual tone of mind and heart). The earnest (heartfelt, continued) prayer of a righteous (one in right standing with God) man (availeth) makes tremendous power available (dynamic in its working).

Jeremiah 17:14 – Heal me, O Lord, and I shall be healed; save me and I shall be saved, for You are my praise!

Romans 4:20 – No unbelief or distrust made him waver (doubtingly question) concerning the promise of God, but he "grew" strong and was empowered by faith as he gave praise and glory to God...

Isaiah 12:5 – Sing praises to the Lord, for He has done excellent things (gloriously); let this be made known to all the earth.

Psalm 96:4 – For great is the Lord and greatly to be praised; He is to be reverently feared and worshiped above all …

Prayer for Healing
Ephesians 4:23 – And be constantly renewed in the spirit of your mind (having a fresh mental and spiritual attitude).

Isaiah 53:5 – He was wounded for our transgressions, He was bruised for our iniquities; the chastisement of our peace was upon Him, and with His stripes we are healed.

Romans 8:10 – But if Christ is in me, the body is dead because of sin, but the Spirit is alive because of righteousness. And if the Spirit of Him who raised Jesus from the dead dwells in me, He who raised Christ from the dead will also give life to my mortal body through the Spirit who dwells in me!

Exodus 23:25-26 – You shall serve the Lord your God, He shall bless your bread and water, and I will take sickness away from the midst of thee…the number of thy days I will fulfill.

Psalm 103:2-3 – Bless the Lord oh my soul and forget not all His benefits; Who forgive all thy iniquities, Who healeth all my diseases.

Jeremiah 30:17 – For I will restore health unto thee, and I will heal thee of thy wounds, saith the Lord.

Psalm 107:20 – He sends forth His word and heals them and rescues them from the pit and destruction.

Psalm 30:2 – O Lord my God, I cried to You and You have healed me.

Mark 10:52 – And Jesus said to him, Go your way; your faith has healed you.

1 Peter 2:24 – He personally bore our sins in His (own) body on the tree (as on an altar and offered Himself on it) that we might die (cease to exist) to sin and live to righteousness. By His wounds you have been HEALED.

Ephesians 3:20 – Now to Him, Who by (in consequence of) the [action of His] power that is at work within us, is able to [carry out His purpose and] do superabundantly, far over and above all that we [dare] ask or think [infinitely beyond our highest prayers, desires, thoughts, hopes or dreams.]

3 John 1:2 – Beloved, I pray that you may prosper in every way and (that your body) may keep well, even as (I know) your soul (your mind, will and emotions) keeps well and prospers.

Healing Communion

Mark 14:22-24 – And while they were eating, He took a loaf (bread), praised God and gave thanks and asked Him to bless it to their use. Then He broke it and gave to them and said, Take. Eat. This is My body. He also took a cup (of juice of grapes) and when He had given thanks, He gave it to them and they all drank of it. And He said to them, This is My blood (which ratifies) the new covenant, (the blood) which is being poured out for many for forgiveness of sins.

1 Corinthians 10:16-17 – The cup of blessing (of wine at the Lord's Supper) upon which we ask (God's) blessing, does it not mean (that in drinking it) we participate in and share a fellowship (a communion) in the blood of Christ (the Messiah)? The bread which we break, does it not mean (that in eating it) we participate in and share a fellowship (a communion) in the body of Christ? For we (no matter how) numerous we are, are one body, because we all partake of the one Bread (the One Whom the communion bread represents).

1 Corinthians 11:23-26 – For I received from the Lord Himself that which I passed on to you, that the Lord Jesus on the night when He was treacherously delivered up and while His betrayal was in progress took bread, and when He had given thanks, He broke it and said, Take, Eat. This is My body, which is broken for you. Do this to call Me (affectionately) to remembrance. For every time you eat this bread and drink this cup, you are representing and

signifying and proclaiming the fact of the Lord's death until He comes (again).

1 Corinthians 11:28 – Let a man (thoroughly) examine himself, and (only when he has done) so should he eat of the bread and drink of the cup.

1 Peter 2:24 – He personally bore our sins in His (own) body on the tree (the cross – as on an altar and offered Himself on it) that we might die (cease to exist) to sin and live to righteousness (in right standing, communion with God). By His wounds you have been healed.

1 John 1:9 – If we (freely) admit that we have sinned and confess our sins, He is faithful and just (true to His own nature and promises) and will forgive our sins (dismiss our lawlessness) and (continuously) cleanse us from all unrighteousness (everything not in conformity to His will in purpose, thought, and action).

Prayer of Intercession for Others
Job 42:10 – And the Lord turned the captivity of Job and restored his fortunes, when he prayed for his friends; also the Lord gave twice as much as he had before.

Romans 8:27 – And He Who searches the hearts of men knows what is in the mind of the (Holy) Spirit, because the Spirit intercedes and pleads (before God) in behalf of the saints …

Isaiah 59:16 – And He (the Lord God) saw that there was no man and wondered that there was no intercessor…

Prayer for Your Husband
Ephesians 4:32 – Be kind to one another, tenderhearted, forgiving one another, even as God in Christ forgave you.

Psalm 90:17 – Let the beauty of the Lord our God be upon us; and establish the works of our hands for us; yes, establish the works of our hands.

Philippians 2:1-2 (KJV) – If there is any consolation in Christ, if any comfort of love, if any fellowship of the Spirit, if any affection and mercy. Fulfill my joy by being like-minded, having the same love, being of one accord, of one mind.

Isaiah 41:10 – Fear not, I am with you; be not dismayed, for I am your God. I will strengthen you, yes, I will help you, I will uphold you with My righteous right hand.

Prayer for Your Children
Psalm 34:11 – Come, you children, listen to me: I will teach you to revere and worshipfully fear the Lord.

Proverbs 14:26 – In the reverent and worshipfully fear of the Lord there is strong confidence and His children shall always have a place of refuge.

Proverbs 20:7 – The righteous man walks in his integrity, blessed (happy, fortunate, and enviable) are his children after him.

Proverbs 31:28 – Her children rise up and call her blessed (happy, fortunate, and to be envied)…

Philippians 1:6 – Being confident of this very thing, that He which hath begun a good work in you will perform it until the day of Jesus Christ.

John 14:13-14 – Whatever you ask in My Name, that I will do, that the Father may be glorified in the Son. If you ask anything in My Name, I will do it.

Prayer for Family Unity
Proverbs 24:3- 4 – Through wisdom a house is built and by understanding it is established, by knowledge the rooms are filled with all precious and pleasant riches.

Acts 16:31 - …Believe in the Lord Jesus Christ (giving yourself up to Him, take yourself out of your own keeping and entrust yourself into His keeping) and you will be saved (and this applies both to) you and your household as well.

Proverbs 13:22 – A good man leaves an inheritance (of moral stability and goodness) to his children's children…

Matthew 18:20 (KJV) – For where two or more are gathered together in My name, there Am I in the midst of them.

Joshua 24:15 - …as for me and my house, we will serve the Lord.

Prayer of Praise
Psalm 22:3 (KJV) – But thou art Holy, O Thou, that inhabits the praises of Israel (His people).

Psalm 18:49 – Therefore will I give thanks and extol You, O Lord, among the nations, and sing praises to Your Name.

2 Samuel 22:4 – I call on the Lord, Who is worthy to be praised, and I am saved from my enemies.

1 Chronicles 16:25 – Great is the Lord and greatly to be praised. He is to be honored, and given glory above all others and above all else.

*I*ncline *Your Ear To Hear and Your Heart To Receive*
Proverbs 4:20-22 – My son, attend to my words, incline thine ear unto My saying. Let them not depart from thine

eyes; keep them in the midst of thine heart. For they are life unto those that find them, and health to all their flesh.

Psalm 10:17 (KJV) – Lord, thou hast heard the desire of the humble; thou wilt prepare their heart, thou wilt cause thine ear to hear.

Psalm 54:2-4 (KJV) – Hear my prayer, O God; give ear to the words of my mouth…Behold, God is mine helper, the Lord is with them that uphold my soul.

Job 22:22 – Receive, I pray you, the law and instruction from His mouth and lay up His words in your heart.

Psalm 51:10 - Create in me a clean heart, O God and renew a right, persevering, and steadfast spirit within me.

Psalm 139:23-24 - Search me (thoroughly), O God, and know my heart! Try me and know my thoughts! And see if there is any wicked or hurtful way in me, and lead me in the way everlasting.

Proverbs 5:1 – My son be attentive to My Wisdom (godly Wisdom learned by actual and costly experience) and incline your ear to My understanding.

Morning Prayer of Encouragement
Psalm 5:3 – In the morning You hear my voice, O Lord; in the morning I prepare (a prayer, a sacrifice) for You and watch and wait (for You to speak to my heart).

Lamentations 3:22-23 – It is because of the Lord's mercy and loving-kindness that we are not consumed, because His (tender) compassions fail not. They are new every morning; great and abundant is Your stability and faithfulness.

Psalm 27:14 – Wait and hope for and expect the Lord; be brave and of good courage and let your heart be stout (bold) and enduring. Yes, wait for and hope for and expect the Lord.

2 Corinthians 1:3-4 – Blessed be the God and Father of our Lord Jesus Christ, the Father of sympathy (pity and mercy) and the God (Who is the Source) of every comfort (consolation and encouragement), Who comforts (consoles and encourages) us in every trouble (calamity and affliction), so that we may also be able to comfort (console and encourage) those who are in any kind of trouble or distress, with the comfort (consolation and encouragement) with which we ourselves are comforted, encouraged by God.

Right Confessions – My Words Shape My Life
Proverbs 18:21 – Death and life are in the power of the tongue, and they who indulge in it shall eat the fruit of it.

Psalm 141:3 – Set a guard, O Lord, before my mouth, keep watch at the door of my lips.

Psalm 30:12 – To the end my tongue and my heart and everything glorious within me may sing praises to You and not be silent. O Lord, my God I will give thanks to You forever.

Proverbs 12:18 – There are those who speak rashly, like the piercing of a sword, but the tongue of the wise brings healing.

1 Peter 3:10 – For let him who wants to enjoy life and see good days keep his tongue free from evil and his lips from deceit.

Philippians 2:11 – And every tongue confess and acknowledge that Jesus Christ is Lord, to the glory of God the Father.

Proverbs 18:20 – A man's (moral) self shall be filled with the fruit of his mouth; and with the consequences of his words he must be satisfied (whether good or bad).

Romans 10:9-10 – …confess with your lips …and in your heart believe…with the heart a person believes…and with the mouth he confesses.

Psalm 63:3 – O Lord open my lips and my mouth shall show forth Your praise.

Prayer for Wisdom and Understanding
Ephesians 1:17 – For I always pray to the God of our Lord Jesus Christ, the Father of glory, that He may grant you a spirit of wisdom and revelation in the knowledge of Him.

Ephesians 1:18 – By having the eyes of your heart flooded with light so that you can know and understand the hope to which He has called you and how rich is His glorious inheritance in the saints (His set apart ones).

James 1:5 – If any of you is deficient in wisdom, let him ask of the giving God (Who gives) to everyone liberally and ungrudging, without reproaching of faultfinding and it will be given him.

Job 12:12-13 – With the aged (you say) is wisdom and with the length of days comes understanding. But only with God are (perfect) wisdom and might; He alone has (true) counsel and understanding.

Grace To Endure

2 Corinthians 12:9 - My grace (My favor and loving-kindness and mercy) is enough for you (sufficient against any danger and enables you to bear the trouble) for My Strength and Power are made perfect (fulfilled and completed) and show themselves most effective in (your) weakness and infirmities, that the strength and power of Christ (the Messiah) may rest (yes, pitch a tent over and dwell) upon you.

Hebrews 4:16 – Let us then fearlessly and confidently and boldly draw near to the throne of grace (the throne of God's unmerited favor) that we may receive mercy (for our failures) and find grace to help in good time for every need (appropriate help and well-timed help, coming just when we need it).

Psalm 121:1-2 – I will lift my eyes to the hills from whence shall my help come. My help comes from the Lord, Who made heaven and earth.

2 Timothy 2:3 – Thou therefore endure hardness, as a good solider of Jesus Christ.

James 4:6 – But He gives more and more grace (power of the Holy Spirit, to meet this evil tendency and all other fully)…God gives grace (continually) to the lowly (those who humble enough to receive it).

Ephesians 1:2 – May grace (God's unmerited favor) and spiritual peace (which means peace with God and harmony, unity, and undisturbness) be yours from God our Father and from the Lord Jesus Christ.

Forgiveness – Healing for the Soul – Overcoming Anger, Bitterness and Offense

Psalm 31:2 -3 – Bow down Your ear to me, deliver me speedily! Be my Rock of refuge, a strong Fortress to save me! Yes, You are my Rock and my Fortress, therefore for Your name's sake lead me and guide me.

Ephesians 4:31-32 – Let all bitterness and indignation and wrath (passion, rage, bad temper) and resentment (anger, animosity) and quarreling… be banished from you… And become useful and helpful and kind to one another, tenderhearted (compassionate, understanding, loving-hearted), forgiving one another (readily and freely), as God in Christ forgave you.

Proverbs 14:29 – He who is slow to anger has great understanding…

James 1:19 – Understand (this), my beloved brethren. Let every man be quick to hear (a ready listener), slow to speak, slow to take offense and to get angry.

Psalm 147:3 – He heals the brokenhearted and binds up their wounds (curing their pains and their sorrows).

Hebrews 12:15 – Exercise foresight and be on the watch to look (after one another), to see no one falls back from and fails to secure God's grace (his unmerited favor and spiritual blessing) in order that no root of resentment (rancor, bitterness, or hatred) shoots forth and causes trouble and bitter torment, and the many become contaminated and defiled by it.

1 Timothy 2:8 – I desire therefore that in every place men should pray, without anger or quarreling or resentment or doubt (in their minds) lifting up holy hands.

Matthew 6:14-15 – For if you forgive people their (offenses) trespasses, (their reckless and willful sins, leaving them, letting them go, and giving up resentment), your Father will also forgive you.

Mark 11:26 – But if you do not forgive, neither will your Father in heaven forgive your failings and shortcomings.

Psalm 4:4 –Be angry but sin not; commune with your own heart (do a self -inventory) upon your bed and be silent (sorry for the things you say in your hearts). Selah (pause, and calmly think of that)!

Proverbs 19:11 – Good sense makes a man restrain his anger and it is his glory to overlook a transgression or an offense.

Ephesians 4:26-27 – When you are angry do not sin; do not ever let your wrath (your exasperation, your fury or indignation) last until the sun goes down. Leave no (such) room or foothold for the devil (give no opportunity to him).

A Heart That Chases After You
Acts 13:22 – I have found David son of Jesse, a man after My own heart; he will do everything I want him to do.

Colossians 3:15 – And let the peace (soul harmony which comes) from Christ rule (act as umpire continually) in your hearts (deciding and settling with finality all questions that arise in your minds, in that peaceful state) to which as (members of Christ's) one body you were also called to live. And be thankful (appreciative), giving praise to God always.

Psalm 24:3-4 – Who shall go up into the mountain of the Lord? Or who shall stand in His Holy Place? He who has clean hands and a pure heart…

Psalm 108:1 – O God, my heart is fixed (steadfast, in the confidence of faith), I will sing, yes, I will sing praises, even with my glory (all the faculties and powers of one created in Your image)!

Psalm 86:12-13 – I will confess and praise You, O Lord my God, with my whole (united) heart; and I will glorify Your name forevermore. For great is Your mercy and loving-kindness toward me; and You have delivered me from the depths of Sheol (from the exceeding depths of affliction).

Joel 2:12 – Therefore, turn to me and keep on coming to Me with all your heart, with fasting, with weeping, and with mourning (until every hindrance is removed and the broken fellowship is restored).

Luke 10:27 – You must love the Lord your God with all your heart and with all your soul and with all your strength and with all your mind and your neighbor as yourself.

Psalm 119:32-34 – I will (not merely walk, but) run the way of Your commandments, when You give me a heart that is willing. Teach me, O Lord, the way of Your statutes and I will keep it to the end (steadfastly). Give me understanding, (in my heart) that I may keep Your law; yes, I will observe it with my whole heart.

Ezekiel 11:19 – And I will give them one heart (a new heart) and I will put a new spirit within them; and I will take the stony (unnaturally hardened) heart out of their flesh and will give them a heart of flesh (sensitive and responsive to the touch of God).

2 Chronicles 19:3 – But there are good things found in you… you have set your heart to seek God (with all your soul's desire).

Jeremiah 29:13 – Then you will seek Me, inquire for, and require Me (as a vital necessity) and find Me when you search for Me with all your heart.

Proverbs 4:23 – Keep and guard your heart with all vigilance and above all that you guard, for out of it flow the springs of life.

You Hear My Prayers
Psalm 4:1 – Answer me when I call, O God of my righteousness (uprightness, justice, and right standing with You)! You have freed me when I was hemmed in and enlarged me when I was in distress; have mercy upon me and hear my prayer.

Exodus 22:27 – When he cries to Me I will hear, for I am gracious and merciful.

Jeremiah 29:12 – Then you will call upon Me and you will come and pray to Me and I will hear and heed you.

Psalm 3:4 – With my voice I cry to the Lord and He hears and answers me out of His holy hill.

Psalm 116:1-2 – I love the Lord, because He has heard (and now hears) my voice and my supplications. Because He has inclined His ear to me, therefore will I call upon Him as long as I live.

Proverbs 15:29 – The Lord is far from the wicked, but He hears the prayer of the (consistently) righteous (the upright, in right standing with Him).

Galatians 4:6 – And because you (really) are (His) sons, God has sent the (Holy) Spirit of His Son into our hearts, crying, Abba (Father)! Father!

*N*ever Stop Believing and Trusting In Him

Matthew 21:22 – And whatever you ask for in prayer, having faith and believing, you will receive.

John 12:44 – But Jesus loudly declared, the one who believes in Me does not (only) believe in and trust in and rely on Me, but (believing in Me he believes) in Him who sent Me.

Psalm 62:5-6 – My soul, wait only upon God and silently submit to Him, for hope and expectation are from Him. He only is my Rock and my Salvation; He is my Defense and my Fortress, I shall not be moved.

James 2:23 – And the Scripture was fulfilled that says, Abraham believed in (adhered to, trusted in, and relied on) God, and this was accounted to him as righteousness (as conformity to God's will in thought and deed) and he was called God's friend.

Psalm 27:13 – What would have become of me had I not believed that I would see the Lord's goodness in the land of the living?

John 2:22 – When therefore He had risen from the dead, His disciples remembered that He said this. And so they believed and trusted and relied on the Scripture and the word (message) Jesus had spoken.

Mark 11:24-25 – For this reason, I am telling you, whatever you ask for in prayer, believe (trust and be confident) that it is granted to you and you will (get it). And whenever you stand praying, if you have anything against anyone, forgive him and let it drop (leave it, let it go) in order that your Father Who is in heaven may also forgive you your (own) failings and shortcomings and let them drop.

1 John 3:23 – And this is His order (His command, His injunction) that we should believe in (put our faith and trust in and adhere to and rely on) the name of His Son Jesus Christ (the Messiah) and that we should love one another, just as He has commanded us.

Hebrews 11:1 – (KJV) – Now faith is the substance of things hoped for the evidence of things not seen.

Mark 2:5 – And when Jesus saw their faith (their confidence in God through Him), He said to the paralyzed man, son, your sins are forgiven (you) and put away (that is, the penalty is remitted, the sense of guilt removed, and you are made upright and in right standing with God).

Expect Your Healing
1 Peter 2:24 –He personally bore our sins in His (own) body on the tree (as on an altar and offered Himself on it), that we might die (cease to exist) to sin and live to righteousness. By His wounds (stripes) you have been healed.

Isaiah 53:5 –But He was wounded for our transgressions, He was bruised for our guilt and iniquities; the chastisement (needful to obtain) of our peace and well-being for us was upon Him, and with the stripes (that wounded) Him we are healed and made whole.

Psalm 25:21 – Let integrity and uprightness preserve me, for I wait for and expect You.

Isaiah 40:31 – But those who wait for the Lord (who expect, look for, and hope in Him) shall change and renew their strength and power; they shall lift their wings and mount up (close to God) as eagles (mount up to the sun); they shall run and not get weary, they shall walk and not faint or become tired.

Psalm 25:5 – Guide me in Your truth and faithfulness and teach me, for You are the God of my salvation; for You (You only and altogether) do I wait (expectantly) all the day long.

Psalm 27:14 – Wait and hope for and expect the Lord; be brave and of good courage and let your heart be stout (brave and bold) and enduring. Yes, wait for and hope for and expect the Lord.

Psalm 25:3 – Yes, let none who trust and wait hopefully and look for You be put to shame or be disappointed…

Romans 8:25 – But if we hope for what is still unseen by us, we wait (anticipate) for it with patience and composure.

Trust In The Lord
Proverbs 3:5-6 – Lean on, trust in, and be confident in the Lord with all your heart and mind and do not rely on your own insight or understanding. In all your ways know, recognize, and acknowledge Him, and He will direct and make straight and plain your path.

Psalm 5:11 – But let all those who take refuge and put their trust in You rejoice; let them ever sing and shout for joy, because You make a covering over them and defend them; let those also who love Your name be joyful in You and be in high spirits.

Psalm 18:2 – The Lord is my Rock, my Fortress, and my Deliverer; my God, my keen and firm Strength in Whom I will trust and take refuge, my Shield, and the horn of my salvation, my High Tower.

Nahum 1:7 – The Lord is good, a Strength and Stronghold in the day of trouble; He knows (recognizes, has knowledge of, and understands) those who take refuge and trust in Him.

Psalm 16:8-10 – I have set the Lord continually before me; because He is at my right hand, I shall not be moved. Therefore my heart is glad and my glory (my inner self) rejoices; my body too shall rest and confidently dwell in safety.

Psalm 46:10 – Let be and be still and know (recognize and understand) that I am God.

Isaiah 12:2 –Behold, God my salvation! I will trust and not be afraid, for the Lord God is my strength and song; yes, He has become my salvation.

Binding the Spirit of Fear
2 Timothy 1:7 – For God did not give us a spirit of fear (timidity), but He has given us a spirit of power and of love and of calm and well-balanced mind and discipline and self-control.

Philippians 4:6 – Do not fret or have any anxiety about anything, but in every circumstance and in everything, by prayer and petition, with thanksgiving, continue to make your request known to God. And God's peace... which transcends all understanding shall garrison and mount guard over your heart and mind in Christ Jesus.

Exodus 14:13-14 – …Fear not; stand still (firm, confident, undismayed) and see the salvation of the Lord which He will work for you today. The Lord will fight for you and you shall hold your peace and remain at rest.

1 John 4:18-19 (KJV) – There is no fear in love; but perfect love casteth out all fear; because fear hath torment. He that feareth is not (yet) made perfect in love. We love Him, because He first loved us.

Hebrews 10:38 – But the just shall live by faith and if he draws back and shrinks in fear, My soul has no delight or pleasure in him.

Take Courage
Matthew 9:21-22 – For she kept saying to herself, if I only touch His garment I shall be restored to health. Jesus turned around and seeing her, He said Take courage daughter! Your faith has made you well. And at once the woman was restored to health.

Nehemiah 4:14 – … Do not be afraid of the enemy (earnestly) remember the Lord and imprint Him (on your minds) great and terrible and take from Him courage to fight…

Psalm 31:24 – Be strong and let your heart take courage, all you that wait for and hope for and expect the Lord!

Joshua 1:9 – Be strong, vigorous, and very courageous. Be not afraid, neither be dismayed, for the Lord your God is with you wherever you go.

Matthew 9:2 – …when Jesus saw their faith, He said…Take courage, your sins are forgiven and the penalty remitted.

Psalm 18:2 – The Lord is my Rock, my Fortress, and my Deliverer; my God, my keen and firm Strength in whom I will trust and take refuge, my Shield and the Horn of my salvation, my High Tower.

2 Corinthians 7:4 – I have great boldness and free and fearless confidence and cheerful courage toward you…

Joshua 10:25 – …Fear not nor be dismayed; be strong and of good courage.

Ezra 10:4 – Be strong and brave and do it.

Cast Your Cares
1 Peter 5:7 – Casting the whole of your care, (all your anxieties and all your worries, all your concerns once and for all) on Him for He cares for you affectionately and cares about you watchfully.

Ezekiel 18:31 – Cast away from you all your transgressions by which you have transgressed against Me, and make you a new mind and heart and a new spirit.

Matthew 11:28-30 – (KJV) – Come onto Me all ye that labour and are heavy laden and I will give you rest. Take My yoke (cast your yoke, burden, cares onto Me and take up Mine) upon you and learn of Me; for I Am meek and lowly in heart and ye shall find rest unto your souls. For My yoke is easy and My burden is light.

Psalm 138:8 – The Lord will perfect that which concerns me; Your mercy and loving-kindness, O Lord, endure forever.

The Joy Of The Lord Is My Strength

Nehemiah 8:10 – And be not grieved and depressed, for the joy of the Lord is your strength and stronghold.

Psalm 13:5 – But I have trusted, leaned on and been confident in Your mercy and loving-kindness; my heart shall rejoice and be in high spirits in Your salvation.

Psalm 16:11 – You will show me the path of life; in Your presence is fullness of joy, at Your right hand there are pleasures forevermore.

Acts 2:28 –You have made known to me the ways of life; You will enrapture me (diffusing my soul with joy) with and in Your Presence.

Psalm 126:5 – They who sow in tears shall reap in joy and singing.

Jeremiah 33:11 – There shall be heard again the voice of joy and the voice of gladness…give thanks to the Lord of host, for the Lord is good; for His mercy and kindness and steadfast love endure forever.

Job 8:21 – He will yet fill your mouth with laughter and your lips with joyful shouting.

Proverbs 17:22 – A happy heart is good medicine and a cheerful mind works healing.

Proverbs 15:13 – A glad heart makes a cheerful countenance.

Jeremiah 15:16 –…Your words were to me a joy and the rejoicing of my heart, for I am called by Your name.

I Am An Overcomer
John 16:33 – For I have overcome the world (I have deprived it of power to harm you and have conquered it for you).

1 John 5:4 – For whatsoever is born of God overcometh the world; and this is the victory that overcometh the world, even our faith.

Revelation 12:11 – And they overcame by the blood of the Lamb and by the word of their testimony…

2 Corinthians 2:14 (KJV) – Now thanks be unto God, Who always causeth us to triumph in Christ.

Romans 8:37 – Yet amid all these things we are more than conquerors and gain a surpassing victory through Him Who loved us.

*K*now He Will Never Leave You Nor Forsake You
Joshua 1:9 – Be not afraid, neither be dismayed, for the Lord your God is with you wherever you go.

1 Chronicles 28:20 – Fear not, be not dismayed, for the Lord, my God, is with you.

John 14:18 (KJV) – I will not leave you comfortless; I will come to you.

John 14:27 – Do not let your hearts be troubled, neither let them be afraid.

1 Samuel 12:22 – The Lord will not forsake His people for His great name's sake, for it has pleased Him to make you a people for Himself.

Psalm 46:1 – GOD is our Refuge and Strength (mighty and impenetrable to temptation) a very present and well-proved help in time of trouble.

When I'm Weary
Isaiah 40:28-29 – The everlasting God, the Lord, the Creator of the ends of the earth, does not faint or grow weary…He gives power to the faint and weary and to him who has no might He increases strength.

Isaiah 40:31 – But those who wait for the Lord (who expect, look for and hope in Him) shall change and renew their strength and power; they lift their wings and mount up (close to God) as eagles; they shall run and not be weary, they shall walk and not faint or become tired.

Matthew 11:28-29 – Come to Me, all you who labor and are heavy-laden and overburdened and I will cause you to rest.

Psalm 23:2 (KJV) – He restoreth my soul, He leadeth me in the paths of righteousness for His name's sake.

Proverbs 17:22 – A happy heart is good medicine and a cheerful mind works healing…

Psalm 103:2 – Bless the LORD, O my soul, and forget not all His benefits; who forgives all your iniquities, Who heals all your disease…

James 5:15 – And the prayer (that is) of faith will save him who is sick and the Lord will restore him; and if he has committed sins, he will be forgiven.

2 Thessalonians 3:13 – …Do not become weary or lose heart in doing right but continue in well-doing without weakening.

Breaking Generational Curses
Exodus 20:5-6 – Thou shall not bow down thyself to them, nor serve them, for I the Lord thy God am a jealous God, visiting the iniquity of the fathers upon the children unto the third and fourth generation of them that hate Me; And showing mercy unto thousands of them that love Me, and keep My commands.

Deuteronomy 5:10 – And (the Lord) showing mercy and steadfast love to thousands and to a thousand generations of those who love Me and keep My commandments.

John 14:15 – If you love Me, keep My commandments.

Isaiah 41:4 – Who has prepared and done this, calling forth and guides the destinies of the generations from the beginning? I, the Lord –the first (existing before history began) and with the last (an ever-present, unchanging God) –I am He.

John 8:36 – Who the Son sets free is free indeed.

Proverbs 26:2 (KJV) - As the bird by wandering, as the swallow by flying, so a curse causeless (without a cause) shall not come.

Ezekiel 18:14 – If, however he begets a son who sees all the sins which his father has done, and considers but does not do likewise…but has executed My judgments and walked in My statutes. He shall not die for the iniquity of his father; he shall surely live.

Resting In the Lord
Psalm 37:7 – Be still and rest in the Lord; wait for Him and patiently lean yourself upon Him…

Hebrews 4:9 (KJV) – There remaineth therefore a rest to the people of God. For he that entered into His (God's) rest, he also hath ceased from his own works, as God did from His.

Psalm 16:8-9 – I have set the Lord continually before me; because He is at my right hand, I shall not be moved. Therefore my heart is glad and my glory (my inner self) rejoices; my body too shall rest and confidently dwell in safety…

Psalm 131:1-2 – LORD, my heart is not haughty, nor my eyes lofty; neither do I exercise myself in matters too great or in things too wonderful (high) for me. Surely I have calmed and quieted my soul, like a child weaned with his mother, like a weaned child is my soul within me (ceased from fretting).

Job 19:25 – For I know that my Redeemer and Vindicator lives…

Maintaining Your Healing
Proverbs 4:4 – Let your heart hold fast My words; keep may commandments and live.

Hosea 12:6 – Therefore return to your God! Hold fast to love and mercy, to righteousness and justice, and wait (expectantly) for your God continually!

Hebrews 4:14 – Inasmuch then as we have a great High Priest Who has ascended and passed through the heavens, Jesus the Son of God, let us hold fast our confession (of faith in Him).

Revelation 2:25-26 – Only hold fast to what you have until I come. And he who overcomes (is victorious) and who obeys My commands to the (very) end (doing the works that please Me), I will give him authority and power over the nations.

Job 19:25 – For I know my Redeemer and Vindicator lives and at last He (the Last One) will stand upon the earth.

James 5:16 (KJV) – The effectual fervent prayer of the righteous availeth much.

I Thessalonians 5:17 – Be unceasing in prayer (praying perseveringly); Thank (God) in everything (no matter what the circumstances may be, be thankful and give thanks), for this is the will of God for you (who are) in Christ Jesus (the Revealer and Mediator of that will).

James 4:7-8 (KJV) – Submit yourselves therefore to God. Resist the devil, and he will flee from you. Draw nigh to God, and He will draw nigh to you.

And when Jesus saw her, He called her to Him and said unto her, woman thou art loosed from thine infirmity!

Luke 13:12 (KJV)